TERTULLIAN'S TRACT
ON THE PRAYER

Q. SEPTIMII FLORENTIS TERTULLIANI
DE ORATIONE LIBER

TERTULLIAN'S TRACT
ON
THE PRAYER

The Latin text with critical notes,
an English translation, an introduction,
and explanatory observations

BY

ERNEST EVANS

D.D. Oxford, Hon. D.D. Glasgow
Vicar of Hellifield, and
Canon of Bradford

LONDON
S·P·C·K
1953

CAMBRIDGE UNIVERSITY PRESS
Cambridge, New York, Melbourne, Madrid, Cape Town,
Singapore, São Paulo, Delhi, Tokyo, Mexico City

Cambridge University Press
The Edinburgh Building, Cambridge CB2 8RU, UK

Published in the United States of America by Cambridge University Press, New York

www.cambridge.org
Information on this title: www.cambridge.org/9781107601444

© Cambridge University Press 1953

First published 1953
First paperback edition 2011

A catalogue record for this publication is available from the British Library

ISBN 978-1-107-60144-4 Paperback

CONTENTS

FRANCISCAE MARGARITAE

MARGARITAE ELIZABETHAE

CHRISTINAE MARIAE

PREFACE

The Latin text here presented is deliberately conservative. To some extent in this treatise, but still more elsewhere, Tertullian seems to have been even too well served by his editors. The great scholars of the sixteenth and seventeenth centuries, whose immense learning is the admiration of all time, introduced their own conjectures (which have now become the standard text) in places where it seems possible that the manuscripts give not only a tolerable but a preferable reading. There remain, however, a few places whose difficulty has not yet been solved, on some of which I have ventured to make suggestions which I submit to the judgement of the learned.

Professor G. F. Diercks' *grande volumen* came into my hands when my own work was, as I thought, complete. In view of it I have thoroughly revised all I had written. How much I owe to this magnificent work is made abundantly clear in my critical notes. I hope also that my translation will escape the severe censure passed by Professor Diercks on two previous English translations of this book.

The Introduction and Notes are not intended to be exhaustive. They will serve their purpose if they introduce to young students one of the most brilliant and versatile writers of Christian antiquity, a master of Latin prose, and suggest to them the possibility of further studies of the same kind. The general reader also may find some benefit from this very early example of a Christian devotional work, along with an insight into the thought and practice of an ancient Christian community.

E. EVANS

HELLIFIELD
Candlemas 1952

INTRODUCTION

Quintus Septimius Florens Tertullianus was born at Carthage, of heathen parentage, apparently about A.D. 160. Some time about 196 he became a convert to Christianity, and, being (as a practising barrister) a man of excellent education and skilful in the presentation of a case, began almost at once to write in defence of the Faith. His apologetic treatises, in which he protests with earnestness and vigour against the official persecution of Christianity, and defends its reasonableness against the attacks of both Jews and pagans, belong apparently to the three or four years immediately following his conversion. In succeeding years he turned his attention to the defence of the traditional Faith against heretical misunderstandings and perversions, and of established Christian discipline against what he regarded as dangerous relaxations. His writings over a period of perhaps twenty-five years thus deal, in no superficial manner, with every one of the subjects which interested the Church in his day: and as he was (with the doubtful exception of Minucius Felix, who in any case has little to say about Christian theology) the earliest Christian writer of Latin, he is the author (or at least the earliest recorder) of the theological terminology still in use in the Latin-speaking Churches and their vernacular-speaking offspring.

At some time, perhaps ten years after his conversion, Tertullian became interested in Montanism. This movement, which originated in Asia Minor about the year 170, claimed that a new revelation, not subversive of but supplementary to traditional Christianity, had been given through a fresh outpouring of the Holy Spirit upon one Montanus and two women, his companions. To the more serious abnormalities of this sect (which we know of from other informants) Tertullian makes no reference, nor does he seem to have been aware of them: but he was from the first attracted by the rigorism of its disciplinary system, and eventually (perhaps about 213) separated himself from the Church of Carthage and became the hostile critic both of it and of the Church of Rome. He claims however, at all times, that the Montanist revelations in no way contradict the traditional faith, though they do (he says) supply it with additional offensive and defensive armament. Certainly he himself was as orthodox in theology after his departure from the Church as he was while within it.

In spite of this (except for St Cyprian, who valued them highly) his writings were always somewhat under a cloud. They were read, certainly, but were quoted (if at all) with some sort of apology. Their survival through the Middle Ages must be regarded as almost a miracle. Towards the end of the fifth century Pope Gelasius forbade the reading of them, and all copies seem to have disappeared from the libraries of Italy. The few manuscripts of Tertullian which now exist seem to be derived from copies preserved in libraries north of the Alps, one of them once the property of the monastic house of Cluny, and it is not unlikely that it was Bernard of that house who rescued this manuscript from obscurity and supplied transcripts of it to several other houses of that order.

The present treatise depends on three authorities, none of them comprising the entire work. The first printed edition, by Martin Mesnart at Paris in 1545, containing chapters 1–19, was made from a manuscript now lost, but which seems to have been a copy of the already mutilated original of the eleventh-century codex Agobardinus (now at Paris). This, our oldest extant authority, contains a number of Tertullian's works, and of the present treatise chapters 1–20; in the first sentence of chapter 21 the copyist, following his original, which had lost a number of pages, passed on (without apparently noticing any discrepancy) to the middle of a sentence near the beginning of a different work *On the Dress of Women*. The end of the book is known only from a Milanese manuscript, formerly at Bobbio, which contains chapters 9–29, with a separate title and table of contents as though this were a complete work *Concerning Divers Kindred Matters*; the overlap, of course, as well as the concluding chapters, shows that this also is part of the homily or tract *On the Prayer*. This manuscript was discovered by Muratori, and published for the first time at Padua in 1713. Very much of our legacy from both Christian and pagan antiquity depends on such slight threads as these.

The tract or homily *On the Prayer* is among the earliest of Tertullian's writings, those composed while he had not yet become interested in Montanism—far less had taken the decisive step of separation from the Church. The attempt to give a precise date to each one of our author's works is probably bound to fail, there being too few references by which to attach them to contemporary events. It is, however, possible with some plausibility to arrange them in the order in which they were written, and we shall not be far out if we place this present work rather high in the list, among those written during the early years of the third century. It is known to have been preceded by at least one of the two books *On the Dress of Women* (to which he refers in chapter 20) and by most of the apologetic treatises. The contrast between the finished style of these earlier works, and what one cannot but call the unkemptness of some sections of the tract *On the Prayer*, suggests that this is a homily rather than a treatise, and indeed not the homily fully written out, but notes to help the preacher's memory. Also, in these sections, the sequence of ideas is so speedy, and telling thoughts are so briefly alluded to, as to make one wonder whether even the most intelligent of congregations could have picked up the preacher's meaning without a good deal of incidental expansion and explanation. And lastly, the expression 'O blessed ones' seems to suggest the hearers of a sermon rather than the readers of a book, while the concluding doxology also is more common in speech than in writing.

The title of the book, *De Oratione*, means strictly *On the Prayer*, and the reference is in the first instance to the Lord's Prayer. But as the work proceeds, its scope expands, coming to include prayer in general, and private prayers in particular. Again in some sections its subject is the public prayers of the Church, both those which, at the end of the preliminary service of scripture-reading and instruction, and after the departure of the unbaptized and those under discipline, the congregation offered as common prayers for the Church and the world, and that other, which apparently could be referred to *par excellence* as 'the prayer', the prayer of consecration of the Eucharist.

The homily begins, as we have said, with an expository commentary on the Lord's Prayer, on which we may remark that it succeeds in saying the obvious things in the obvious way: yet that if these things were worth saying (as the frequency with which they were repeated by later writers shows that they were) they needed, and no doubt received, more extended and impressive enforcement than is here actually set down (chapters 1–9). Then, after a short transitional passage (chapter 10) on further things which we are authorized to pray for, the homilist considers the conditions of acceptable prayer, namely freedom from resentment and other perturbations of soul (chapters 11 and 12). Next comes a series of observations, for the most part very brief, but in one case exhaustively and systematically planned, on practices and observances connected with the public prayers of the Church (chapters 13–27). Here Tertullian takes the opportunity of riding some of his own favourite hobby-horses, or of arguing against other people who wish to ride theirs, and we may be permitted to doubt whether most of this formed part of the original homily; if it did, we can only say that the preacher allowed himself to digress into subjects which (by contrast with the beginning and the end of the book) are comparatively trivial, and at such length as to overthrow the balance of his sermon and to put its directly religious teaching very much in the shade. We may then perhaps think that this (by far the longest) part of the book records the answers given to questions raised at various times, and was added to the homily on publication. These questions are concerned with:

washing the hands before prayer (13);

lifting up and spreading out the hands during prayer (14);

taking off the overcoat during prayer (15);

sitting down immediately the prayers are ended (16);

moderation of the voice in prayer (17);

the new practice of refusing the kiss of peace at the end of the prayers when a person is keeping a fast of private devotion (18);

those who on station days decline to receive the holy communion for fear of breaking their fast (19);

women's dress (20);

the new claim that growing girls, and women who have made public profession of virginity, need not, like other women, cover their heads during the prayers (21, 22);

the new practice of not kneeling for the Church prayers on Saturdays (23);

the place and time of prayer (24, 25);

prayer with one's guest or one's host (26);

Alleluia, and other ornaments of prayer (27).

Chapters 24-7, which reintroduce the more strictly religious aspect of things, may conceivably have formed part of the original homily, and provide a natural transition towards its concluding paragraphs, in which (chapter 28) the claim is made that the prayer (by which, as an odd phrase or two show, the author here means the eucharistic prayer of consecration) is the 'spiritual sacrifice' of the New Covenant; and the preacher concludes his sermon (chapter 29) with an encomium of the power and efficacy of Christian prayer. Thus the book ends on the high religious and rhetorical level on which it began.

The question has been asked, what were the source or sources from which Tertullian may have derived his exposition of the Lord's Prayer, and the suggestion was made (and was at one time widely accepted) that he was making use of a commentary (now lost) on St Matthew's Gospel which Theophilus of Antioch is known to have written (about A.D. 175). Of this one can but say, first, that it is somewhat precarious to assume a known writer's indebtedness to a work of whose contents we know nothing at all; and that even if the suggestion were accepted, nothing is gained by it and no one is any the wiser. Secondly, the extant writings of Theophilus (namely, a treatise in three books intended to prove that Christianity is in its essence older than the heathen religions and philosophies, and therefore possesses the prerogative of truth) show little kinship either in matter or in manner with this or any other of Tertullian's works. And thirdly, the ideas which Tertullian here suggests are such as might have occurred to anyone of reasonable intelligence, and consequently there is no need to suppose that he borrowed them from anyone at all. Tertullian was one of the ablest men of his generation, Christian or heathen, and was competent to be a lender rather than a borrower of ideas; certainly he was more qualified to teach Theophilus than Theophilus to teach him.

Little more than a generation later, St Cyprian, Bishop of Carthage from 248 to 258, who writes on the same subject, had not only read Tertullian's work, but kept it by him as he wrote. He repeats many of the thoughts here suggested, serving them up in more literary Latin, and with such expansions as to convert sermon notes into a formal treatise. Cyprian, as he himself was proud to say, looked upon Tertullian as his very revered teacher —which was the best of reasons for improving upon his work: and since the master's defection to Montanism caused later generations to regard all his works with suspicion, it was through the disciple that his thoughts on the Lord's Prayer became the common property of Christendom, appearing again and again in later writers, and even in official expositions of liturgical documents.

The text of the Lord's Prayer commented on by Tertullian differs in several minor particulars from any other version known to us, but especially in that he has inverted the order of the second and third clauses. The prayer as he rehearses it is as follows:

Father who art in heaven : hallowed be thy name : thy will be done in heaven and in earth : thy kingdom come : give us to-day our daily bread : forgive us our debts [for] we also forgive our debtors : lead us not into temptation, but remove us from the evil.

That the changed order is not due to a mere slip of memory appears from Tertullian's own argument, in which he shows how the one clause depends on the other, as well as from his recapitulation, where he repeats the words 'name', 'will', 'kingdom', in that order. Complicated theories have been evolved in explanation of this, notably the suggestion that the shorter form of the Prayer given by St Luke (11. 2–4), which was current in the

second century and as late as St Augustine,[1] and is to be found in
the English Revised Version,[2] was variously expanded for Church
purposes independently of St Matthew's fuller version, and that
in one of its forms the clauses appeared in this order. This cannot
be ruled out as impossible: though it is equally possible that the
change of order is due to Tertullian himself, who saw the connexion of thought in this way and altered the text accordingly.
We are not unfamiliar with the minister who alters the Church
Service to suit his own theories: and there was much more
liberty in that respect in the second century than there is supposed
to be now.

Some of the observances and Church usages alluded to in
chapters 13 to 27 call for a few words of explanation.

Concerning the public prayers of the Church, it is to be observed that in the second and third centuries the only regular
Church services were those for the administration of Baptism
and the Eucharist. The former, of course, would only be used as
occasion arose: and there are already indications of a tendency
(at least in the case of adult persons) to confine it to Easter and
Pentecost. The Eucharist, throughout the whole of Christendom,
was celebrated every Sunday, and there was an obligation (as in
theory there still is) on all Christians to be present. What is now
called 'non-communicating attendance' was (except for the
innovation deprecated by Tertullian in chapter 19—and this in
any case does not refer to Sundays) unknown in the early Church:
the supposition was that anyone sufficiently in a state of grace to
be present at the service was spiritually competent to offer his
oblation and to receive the sacrament. A custom strange to our
modern ideas, but in common use in the African Church (and
no doubt some others) in the third century, was for each com-
municant, after receiving the sacrament during the service, to
carry it home (in the species of Bread only) wrapped in a napkin,

---

[1] St Augustine, *Enchiridion* 116, explains how St Luke by his very omissions
reinforces the connexion of the clauses recorded by St Matthew.
[2] Father, hallowed be thy name; thy kingdom come; give us day by day our
daily bread: and forgive us our sins, for we ourselves also forgive everyone that
is indebted to us: and bring us not into temptation.

with the intention of taking a small portion at the beginning of every meal: Tertullian in chapter 19 recommends this as a solution of an unnecessary difficulty which some people were making.[1]

The eucharistic service was in two sections. The first of these, a service of Bible-reading and instruction, might be attended by non-Christians: and at the end of it, after the dismissal of un-baptized persons and those under discipline of penance, the congregation (now exclusively Christian) stood to pray, for the whole state of the Church and the world.[2] The remainder of the service, the Eucharist proper, began with the offertory, each head of a family presenting a loaf of bread and a small flask of wine: its characteristic prayer was the long Prayer of Consecration (known variously as the anaphora, the oblation, or the canon), which at least as early as the third century consisted of thanksgiving, oblation, the memorial of the saving acts of Christ, a prayer for consecration, and an intercession for the Church and its members.[3] This second prayer is referred to by Tertullian in chapter 19 as 'the prayers of the sacrifices', and he probably has it in view in chapter 28, describing it as 'the spiritual oblation' and a 'sacrifice of prayer'.

The original Christian posture in public prayers (copied from Jewish practice) was to stand, especially on Sundays, though apparently on other days (at least in the African Church) the congregation knelt. Tertullian refers in chapter 23 to a small minority who wished to stand on Saturdays as well as Sundays. The general tendency seems to have been in the other direction, for in the fourth century it became necessary for the Council of

---

[1] Elsewhere he uses it as an argument against marriage with heathens: 'What will your husband suspect you are eating at the beginning of every meal?' (*Ad Uxorem* 5.)

[2] A relic of these prayers still stands in the Latin Mass: see a note on § 18.

[3] This intercession is for the Church alone, and not for those without. During the 1914–18 war the practice was introduced of interpolating references to various mundane matters before the Prayer for the Church. The place for such things is after the Creed (see the previous note): the Church rule is that after the Offertory the world is shut out and only the People of God prayed for.

Nicaea (325) to forbid kneeling in church at least on Sundays and on the fifty days between Easter and Pentecost.[1]

We have said that the Eucharistic service was divided into two parts, of which the second began with the offertory. Actually the end of the first part or the beginning of the second was marked by the ceremony of the kiss of peace (often referred to briefly as the *pax*), an act and token of Christian fellowship. Its justification, if any had been needed, would have been found in the apostolic injunction, 'Greet ye one another with a holy kiss.'[2] Tertullian refers to this in chapter 18. When he calls the *pax* the seal of the prayer he apparently regards it as the conclusion of the first set of prayers, those for the Church and the world; others regard it as the beginning of the Offertory, and both may be right.

On Sundays, as we have remarked, there was a general obligation to be present at the Eucharist. In Africa, in the third century, as in Egypt in the fourth, Saturdays also were liturgical days. In Rome it seems probable that from the beginning the Eucharist might be celebrated on any day. Wednesdays and Fridays in each week were fast days, though apparently only Good Friday ('the day of the Passover', chapter 18) was a fast of universal obligation: it was not unknown for individuals to undertake a fast of private devotion. The so-called 'station days' were fasts of public, though not of obligatory, observance: they apparently began

---

[1] The Eastern Churches retain the custom of standing. In the West the custom was lost in the Middle Ages, when the congregation, instead of taking notice of the action of the service, engaged (either in polite conversation or) in their own private devotions, for which they knelt down. At the Reformation the Church of England, for local reasons, retained the practice of kneeling for prayer: the continental Reformed Churches reintroduced standing, which is still their custom. In the established Church of Scotland standing was the rule until, within living memory, congregations took to crouching forward on their seats in imitation of English Nonconformists.

[2] The above was the position of the *pax*, in all Churches of which we have information, at the beginning of the third century. At some time before the end of the fourth century the Roman Church transferred the ceremony to the end of the Canon, just before the Communion, where it still remains.

with an all-night vigil, and ended with the Eucharist, or at least the first or the second part of it. Tertullian derives the expression from the military term *statio*, which means the sentinel's turn of duty: others suggest that there was a procession from one church to others, and that 'station' indicates the pause at each of them—though this could hardly have been possible in times of persecution or until there came to be many churches within a small radius, so that probably Tertullian is right.

Towards the end of chapter 22 Tertullian refers to certain women who have made a profession of life-long virginity. This was a practice highly approved of in Christian circles—though exceptionally offensive to both the Jewish and the pagan mind. Such women continued to live an ordinary life in their father's house, and it is Tertullian's claim that they ought to be in no way distinguishable in dress or deportment from other women of their age. Actually it was not long before they obtained such privileges as a special place in church: though it was not until late in the fourth century that they began to live together under the rule of a superior.

From all this it appears that this short book, besides what it may suggest of help in the way of godliness, gives an insight into the mind of a man of strong opinions who was not afraid to express them, as also into the life of a community some at least of whom were not indisposed to make experiments, however little their mentor is prepared to afford them encouragement. The time was soon to come when he, as a Montanist, was to try to enforce many new practices, on the ground that, 'Our Lord Jesus Christ said, "I am the truth", not "I am the custom"'.

MANUSCRIPTS AND EDITIONS

A   *Codex Agobardinus,* formerly the property of Agobard, Bishop of Lyons (816–840), now at Paris (B.N. fonds latin 1622). Contains §§1–20. At §21, *per ecclesias quas,* the copyist, not observing that a number of pages had disappeared from his original, passed on with no break to *De Cult. Fem.* i. 5, *disposita utensilitas.*

B   The *editio princeps,* by Martin Mesnart, Paris, 1545. Contains §§1–19. The rest was either missing from the editor's manuscript, or was omitted as being imperfect. This manuscript was evidently copied from the already mutilated archetype of *A.*

D   *Codex Ambrosianus* (G. 58), ninth or tenth century: formerly at Bobbio. It begins at §9, with the title INC. TERTULLIANI DIVERSARUM RERUM NECESSARIARUM and an index of subjects. In the latter part of the treatise, where *A* and *B* fail, it is the sole authority.

EDITORS

Gel.   Sigismundus Gelenius, Basel, 1550, claims to have had access to many manuscripts, one of them, by far the most accurate, fetched from the far end of Britain. But it does not appear whether the present treatise was in any of these authorities.

Pam.   Jacobus Pamelius, Antwerp, 1579.

Jun.   Franciscus Junius, Franeker, 1597.

Rig.   Nicolaus Rigaltius, Paris, 1634.

Mur.   The edition of L. A. Muratori, Padua, 1713, who discovered *D* and introduced many of his own conjectures. For the latter part of the work this ranks as *editio princeps.*

Routh   M. J. Routh, Oxford, 1832.

Oeh.   Franciscus Oehler, Leipsic, 1853.

Reiff.   Augustus Reifferscheid, Vienna, 1890.

Diercks G. F. Diercks, Bussum, 1947.

Other notes and conjectures

Lat.   Latinus Latinius, Rome, 1583.

Scal.   Joseph Scaliger, in the margin of a copy of Junius, kept in the University Library at Leiden.

Urs.   Fulvius Ursinus, Frankfort, 1603.

x   One or more unnamed scholars in *Miscellaneae Observationes*, Amsterdam, 1733.

Hartel William Hartel, Vienna, 1890.

Kroy.   Aemilius Kroymann, Innsbruck, 1894.

In the Latin text, italics or pointed brackets ⟨ ⟩ indicate conjectures for which there is no MS. authority: square brackets [ ] indicate words which should probably be omitted.

In the translation, pointed brackets serve the same purpose as italics in the English Bible; italics are used here for scriptural quotations.

DE ORATIONE LIBER

Q. SEPTIMII FLORENTIS TERTULLIANI
DE ORATIONE LIBER

1 Dei spiritus et dei sermo et dei ratio, sermo rationis et ratio sermonis et spiritus utrumque, Iesus Christus dominus noster, novis discipulis novi testamenti novam orationis formam determinavit. oportebat enim in hac quoque specie novum vinum
5 novis utribus recondi et novam plagulam novo adsui vestimento. ceterum quicquid retro fuerat, aut demutatum est ut circumcisio aut suppletum ut reliqua lex aut impletum ut prophetia aut perfectum ut fides ipsa. omnia de carnalibus in spiritalia renovavit nova dei gratia superducto evangelio expunctore totius retro
10 vetustatis, in quo et dei spiritus et dei sermo et dei ratio approbatus est dominus noster Iesus Christus, spiritus quo valuit, sermo quo docuit, ratio quo ⟨inter⟩venit. sic oratio a Christo instituta ex tribus constituta est, ex sermone quo enuntiatur, ex spiritu quo tantum potest⟨, ex ratione quo reconciliat⟩. docuerat et Ioannes
15 discipulos suos adorare: sed omnia Ioannis Christo praestruebantur donec ipso aucto (sicut idem Ioannes praenuntiabat illum augeri oportere, se vero deminui) totum praeministri opus cum ipso spiritu transiret ad dominum. ideo nec exstat in quae verba docuerit Ioannes adorare, quod terrena caelestibus cesserint:
20 Qui de terra est, inquit, terrena fatur, et qui de caelis adest, quae vidit ea loquitur: et quid non caeleste quod domini Christi est, ut haec quoque orandi disciplina? consideremus itaque, benedicti, caelestem eius sophiam, imprimis de praecepto secrete adorandi,

---

1: 2 *utrumque AB* utriusque *x, quem sequuntur Reiff., Diercks, male, quantum mihi videtur, intellecto scriptoris sensu: si quid tamen mutandum foret,* utrimque *mallem scripsisse.*

3 novis *Pam.* nobis *AB.*

12 quo (*tertia vice*) *AB* qua *edd. post Lat.* intervenit *scripsi* venit *AB* (*mendum latere suspicantur edd.*) instituta *x* constituta *AB* (*utraque vice*).

14 quo reconciliat *scripsi* ex ratione qua docetur *supplevit Pam.:* pro docetur *maluit Rig.* suscipitur.

TERTULLIAN ON THE PRAYER

1   God's Spirit and God's Word and God's Reason, the Word of the Reason and the Reason of the Word, and both of these Spirit, Jesus Christ our Lord, has marked out for the new disciples of the new covenant a new plan of prayer. For it was right that in this case, too, new wine should be stored in new bottles and a new patch be stitched on to a new garment.[1] For everything that was aforetime has either been transmuted, like circumcision, or supplemented, like the rest of the Law, or fulfilled, like prophecy, or made perfect, like faith itself. The new grace of God has renewed all things from carnal to spiritual by the subsequent addition of the Gospel, the fulfiller of all older antiquity: for in it our Lord Jesus Christ is approved as God's Spirit and God's Word and God's Reason—Spirit in view of his power, Word in view of his teaching, Reason in view of his intervention.   So therefore the prayer instituted by Christ is of three constituents, of word in that it is clearly spoken, of spirit in that it has great power, of reason in that it reconciles. John also had taught his disciples to pray.[2] But all John's acts were laid as foundation for Christ, until, he being increased (as the same John foretold that *He must increase but I must decrease*),[3] the whole work of the forerunner, with the Spirit too, should pass over to the Lord.[4] Consequently it is not even on record according to what formula John taught them to pray, because earthly things have given way to heavenly (*He that is from the earth*, he says, *speaketh earthly things, and he who is come from heaven, what things he hath seen, those he speaketh*),[5] and everything which belongs to the Lord Christ is heavenly, as is also this science of praying.   Let us take note therefore, O blessed ones, of his heavenly wisdom, in the first place regarding the precept of praying in secret,[6] by which he not only made demands upon

---

[1] Matt. 9. 17; Mark 2. 22; Luke 5. 37.   [2] Luke 11. 1.
[3] John 3. 30.   [4] Cf. 2 Kings 2. 15.   [5] Cf. John 3. 31, 32.   [6] Matt. 6. 6.

quo et fidem hominis exigebat, ut dei omnipotentis et conspectum
25 et auditum sub tectis et in abditum etiam adesse confideret, et
modestiam fidei desiderabat, ut quem ubique audire et videre
fideret ei soli religionem suam offerret. sequente sophia in
sequenti praecepto proinde pertineat ad fidem et modestiam
fidei, si non agmine verborum adeundum putemus ad dominum,
30 quem ultro suis prospicere certi sumus. et tamen brevitas ista,
quod ad tertium sophiae gradum faciat, magnae ac beatae inter-
pretationis substantia fulta est, quantumque substringitur verbis
tantum diffunditur sensibus. neque enim propria tantum orationis
officia complexa est, vel venerationem dei aut hominis petitionem,
35 sed omnem paene sermonem domini, omnem commemorationem
disciplinae, ut re vera in oratione breviarium totius evangelii
comprehendatur.

2 Incipit a testimonio dei et merito fidei cum dicimus, PATER
QUI IN CAELIS ES. nam et deum oramus, et fidem commendamus cuius meritum est haec appellatio. scriptum est, Qui in eum
crediderunt, dedit eis potestatem ut filii dei vocentur: quanquam
5 frequentissime dominus patrem nobis pronuntiavit deum, immo
et praecepit ne quem in terris patrem vocemus, nisi quem habemus
in caelis. itaque sic adorantes etiam praeceptum obimus. felices
qui patrem agnoscunt: hoc est quod Israeli exprobratur, quod
caelum ac terram spiritus contestatur, Filios, dicens, genui et illi
10 me non agnoverunt. dicendo autem patrem, deum quoque
cognominamus: appellatio ista et pietatis et potestatis est. item
in patre filius invocatur: Ego, enim inquit, et pater unum sumus.
ne mater quidem ecclesia praeteritur, siquidem in filio et patre
mater recognoscitur, de qua constat et patris et filii nomen. uno
15 igitur genere aut vocabulo et deum cum suis honoramus et
praecepti meminimus et oblitos patris denotamus.

1: 25 in abditis Gel. (contra consuetudinem scriptoris).
   26 modestiam A   modestum B.
   27 sequente AB   sequens Jun.   omisit Diercks.
   28 proinde AB edd.   perinde Reiff., sicut alibi saepius.
   34 vel del. Gel. Reiff.: tuentur Hoppe, Diercks.
2:   4 crediderunt A   crediderint B.

man's faith, that he should trust that the sight and hearing of God Almighty are present within the house and even in the hidden chamber, but also asked for faith's self-restraint, that he should offer his devotion to him alone whom he should believe to have ears and eyes in every place. As a second ⟨degree of⟩ wisdom, in the precept that follows let it likewise pertain to faith and to faith's self-restraint if we suppose we ought not to draw near to the Lord with an army of words,[1] being sure that he provides for his own even without their asking. Yet that brevity (and let this serve for a third degree of wisdom) rests upon the foundation of a great and fruitful interpretation, and in proportion as it is restrained in wording, so is it copious in meaning. For it embraces not merely the particular functions of prayer, be it the worship of God or man's petition, but as it were the whole of the Lord's discourse, the whole record of his instruction: so that without exaggeration there is comprised in the prayer an epitome of the entire Gospel.

2 It begins with ⟨our⟩ bearing witness to God, and with a work of faith, when we say FATHER WHO ART IN HEAVEN: for we are at once praying to God and confessing our faith, since this form of address is a work of faith. It is written, *To them that have believed in him he hath given power to be called sons of God.*[2] And for that matter, the Lord frequently declared that God is to us a father— nay more, he commanded us not to call anyone father upon earth, but only him who is ours in heaven.[3] And so when we pray in these terms, we are also keeping ⟨his⟩ commandment. Happy are they that acknowledge the Father. This it is that Israel is re- proached with: because the Spirit calls heaven and earth to wit- ness, saying, *I have begotten sons and they have not acknowledged me.*[4] But when we say *Father* we also give God a name: this form of address involves both affection and authority. Also in ⟨the title⟩ *Father* we call upon the Son: for he says, *I and the Father are one.*[5] Even our mother the Church is not omitted, seeing that in 'son' and 'father' there is a recognition of 'mother': for the name of both father and son has its actuality from her. Thus under one generic term we both honour God, along with those that are his,

[1] Matt. 6. 7, 8.   [2] Cf. John 1. 12.
[3] Matt. 23. 9.   [4] Cf. Isa. 1. 2.   [5] John 10. 30.

3   Nomen dei patris nemini proditum fuerat: etiam qui de ipso interrogaverat Moyses aliud quidem nomen audierat. nobis revelatum est in filio: *iam* enim filius no*vum* patris nomen est— Ego veni, inquit, in nomine patris: et rursus, Pater glorifica
5 nomen tuum: et apertius, Nomen tuum manifestavi hominibus. id ergo ut sanctificetur postulamus. non quod deceat homines bene deo optare, quasi sit et alius de quo ei possit optari, aut laboret nisi optemus. plane benedici deum omni loco ac tempore condecet ob debitam semper memoriam beneficiorum eius ab
10 omni homine. sed et hoc benedictionis vice fungitur. ceterum quando non sanctum et sanctificatum est per semetipsum nomen dei, cum ceteros sanctificet ex semetipso, cui illa angelorum circumstantia non cessant dicere, Sanctus sanctus sanctus? proinde igitur et nos, angelorum si meruerimus candidati, iam hinc
15 caelestem illam in deum vocem et officium futurae claritatis ediscimus. hoc quantum ad gloriam dei. alioquin, quantum ad nostram petitionem, cum dicimus, SANCTIFICETUR NOMEN TUUM, id petimus ut sanctificetur in nobis qui in illo sumus, simul et in ceteris quos adhuc gratia dei exspectat, ut et huic
20 praecepto pareamus orandi pro omnibus, etiam pro inimicis nostris: ideoque suspensa enuntiatione non dicentes, Sanctificetur in nobis, 'in omnibus' dicimus.

4   Secundum hanc formam subiungimus, FIAT VOLUNTAS TUA IN CAELIS ET IN TERRA: non quod aliquis obsistat quominus voluntas dei fiat, et ei successum voluntatis suae oremus; sed in omnibus petimus fieri voluntatem eius. ex interpretatione enim
5 figurata carnis et spiritus nos sumus caelum et terra. quanquam,

3: 3 iam enim filius novum *Gel.* I. quis enim filius non *A, unde Reiff. extraxit* iam quis enim filius? novum etc. iam enim filius non *B* (*quod scriptoris sententiae manifeste adversatur*) prius enim quam filius non patris nomen est *Diercks.*
4, 5 Ego veni...nomen tuum *om. B.*
13 cessant *A Diercks* cessat *B Reiff.*
14 meruerimus *AB* meminerimus *Gel.* (*perperam*).
20 orandi *x* orando *AB Reiff. Diercks.*   *quaero an* legendum et hic prae-cepto...orando.

and are mindful of the commandment, and pass censure on those who have forgotten the Father.

3 The name of God the Father had been revealed to no man. Even Moses, who had expressly asked concerning it, got his answer, but by another name.[1] To us it has been revealed in the Son. For we know that the Son is the Father's new name: *I am come*, he says, *in the Father's name*:[2] and again, *Father, glorify thy name*:[3] and, more openly, *I have manifested thy name to men*.[4] That therefore is the name we ask should be hallowed. Not that it is seemly for men to wish God well, as though there were another from whom it were possible to wish him ⟨well⟩, or as though he were in difficulties unless we so wish. Of course it is very seemly that God should be well spoken of at every place and time by every man, with a view to that remembrance of his benefits that is always due: and this ⟨clause⟩ does also serve the function of well-speaking. Yet when is the name of God not holy and hallowed ⟨even⟩ of itself, seeing he hallows others from within himself, and those angels that stand around cease not to say to him, *Holy, holy, holy*?[5] Consequently therefore we also, angels-designate[6] if such our merits are found to be, already here are learning ⟨to use⟩ that heavenly address to God and that service of the glory that is to be. Thus far as concerns the glory of God. Besides this, as concerns our own petition: when we say HALLOWED BE THY NAME, our petition is for it to be hallowed in us who are in him, and at the same time also in the rest whom as yet the grace of God is looking out for, so that we obey this precept besides, of praying for all, even for our enemies.[7] And consequently as, with indeterminate expression, we say not 'hallowed in us', we do succeed in saying, 'in all ⟨men⟩'.

4 After this model we subjoin, THY WILL BE DONE IN HEAVEN AND IN EARTH. Not that someone is opposing the will of God being done, and that we are praying on his behalf that his will may prosper: but we ask for his will to be done in all ⟨men⟩. For by the figurative interpretation of flesh and spirit heaven and earth

[1] Ex. 3. 14, 15. [2] John 5. 43. [3] John 12. 28.
[4] John 17. 6. [5] Isa. 6. 3; Rev. 4. 8.
[6] Cf. Matt. 22. 30; Luke 20. 36. [7] Cf. Matt. 5. 44.

etsi simpliciter intellegendum est, idem tamen est sensus petitionis,
ut in nobis fiat voluntas dei in terris, ut possit scilicet fieri et in
caelis. quid autem deus vult quam incedere nos secundum suam
disciplinam? petimus ergo substantiam et facultatem voluntatis
10 suae subministret nobis ut salvi simus et in caelis et in terris, quia
summa est voluntatis eius salus eorum quos adoptavit. est et illa
dei voluntas quam dominus administravit praedicando operando
sustinendo: si enim ipse pronuntiavit non suam sed patris facere
se voluntatem, sine dubio quae faciebat ea erant voluntas patris:
15 ad quae nunc nos velut ad exemplaria provocamur, ut et praedi-
cemus et operemur et sustineamus ad mortem usque: quae ut
implere possimus opus est dei voluntate. item dicentes, Fiat
voluntas tua, vel eo nobis bene optamus quod nihil mali sit in
dei voluntate, etiam si quid pro meritis cuiusque secus inrogatur.
20 iam hoc dicto ad sufferentiam nosmetipsos praemonemus.
dominus quoque cum substantia passionis infirmitatem carnis
demonstrare iam in sua carne voluisset, Pater, inquit, transfer
poculum istud: et recordatus, Nisi quod mea non sed tua fiat
voluntas. ipse erat voluntas et potestas patris, et tamen ad demon-
25 strationem sufferentiae debitae voluntati se patris tradidit.

5 VENIAT quoque REGNUM TUUM ad id pertinet quod et Fiat
voluntas tua, 'in nobis' scilicet: nam deus quando non regnat,
in cuius manu cor omnium regum est? sed quicquid nobis optamus
in illum auguramur, et illi deputamus quod ab illo expectamus.
5 itaque si ad dei voluntatem et ad nostram suspensionem pertinet
regni dominici repraesentatio, quomodo quidam protractum
quendam saeculo postulant, cum regnum dei, quod ut adveniat
oramus, ad consummationem saeculi tendat? optamus maturius

4: 19 secus *AB*   sequius *Scal.* (*perperam*).
  21 substantia *AB Oeh.*   sub instantiam *Urs. Reiff. Diercks.*
5: 1 quod et *AB*   quo et *Leopoldus, Oeh. Reiff. Diercks*   quod est *Semler
  Codd.* tamen *MSS. lectio restituatur, si quidem scribere possis aut eo* pertinet
  quo *aut* ad id pertinet quod, *locutiones vero contaminare vix liceat.*
  6 protractum *A*   pertractum *B*   per tractum *Scal. Reiff.* (*quod quid sibi
  velit nescio*).
  7 saeculo *A*   in saeculo *B edd. paene omnes.*

means us. Although even if it is to be understood literally, yet is the meaning of the petition the same, that in us the will of God may be done in earth—so that it may be possible, of course, for it also to be done in heaven. For what is more God's will than that we should walk according to his instructions? We ask then for him to supply us with the substance and effect of his will, that we may be saved both in heaven and in earth: because the sum-total of his will is the salvation of those he has made his children. There is also that will of God which the Lord administered by preaching and working ⟨miracles⟩ and suffering: for as he himself declared that he was doing not his own will but the Father's,[1] doubtless the things he was doing were the Father's will—things to which as examples we are now challenged, that we should both preach and work and suffer, even unto death. And for us to be able to fulfil these, there is need of God's will. Also, in saying *Thy will be done*, we wish well for ourselves on this ground also, that there is no evil in God's will, even if according to each man's merits something of the other sort is being inflicted. In fact, by saying this we forewarn ourselves with a view to endurance: for when it had now become our Lord's will by the suffering of the passion to display in his own flesh the infirmity of flesh, he said, *Father, remove this cup*, and, recollecting himself, *except that not my will but thine be done*.[2] He himself was the will and the power of the Father, and yet, so as to exemplify the endurance that was due, he surrendered himself to the Father's will.

5   Also, THY KINGDOM COME has the same pertinence as *Thy will be done*—in us, of course. For when is God not the King, seeing that in his hand is the heart of all kings?[3] But whatever it is we choose for ourselves we express with reference to him, and reckon to his account that which we look for from him. And so, if the open manifestation of the Lord's kingdom pertains to God's will and to our expectation, how do certain persons ask for what they call a prolongation for the world, when the kingdom of God, which we pray may come, is directed towards the consummation of the world? Our desire is to reign the

[1] John 6. 37–39.
[2] Matt. 26. 39; Mark 14. 36; Luke 22. 42.   [3] Cf. Prov. 21. 1.

regnare et non diutius servire: etiam si praefinitum in oratione
10 non esset de postulando regni adventu, ultro eam vocem protulissemus festinantes ad spei nostrae complexum. clamant ad
dominum invidia animae martyrum sub altari, Quonam usque
non ulcisceris, domine, sanguinem nostrum de incolis terrae?
nam utique ultio illorum a saeculi fine dirigitur. immo quam
15 celeriter veniat, domine, regnum tuum, votum Christianorum,
confusio nationum, exultatio angelorum, propter quod conflicta-
mur, immo potius propter quod oramus.

6 Sed quam eleganter divina sapientia ordinem orationis instru-
xit, ut post caelestia, id est post dei nomen dei voluntatem et dei
regnum, terrenis quoque necessitatibus petitioni locum faceret:
nam et edixerat dominus, Quaerite prius regnum, et tunc vobis
5 etiam haec adicientur. quanquam PANEM NOSTRUM QUOTI-
DIANUM DA NOBIS HODIE spiritaliter potius intellegamus.
Christus enim panis noster est, quia vita Christus et vita panis:
Ego sum, inquit, panis vitae: et paulo supra, Panis est sermo dei
vivi qui descendit de caelis: tum quod et corpus eius in pane
10 censetur, Hoc est corpus meum. itaque petendo panem quoti-
dianum perpetuitatem postulamus in Christo et individuitatem
a corpore eius. sed et quia carnaliter admittitur ista vox non sine
religione potest fieri et spiritalis disciplinae: panem enim peti
mandat, quod solum fidelibus necessarium est: cetera enim nationes
15 requirunt. ita et exemplis inculcat et parabolis retractat cum dicit,
Numquid panem filiis pater aufert et canibus tradit? item, Numquid filio panem poscenti lapidem tradit? ostendit enim quid

---

5: 10 protulissemus *Rig.* postulissemus *A* postulassemus *B*.

12 invidia *AB* ad domini iudicia *Hartelius: alii alia citra necessitatem tenta-*
verunt: cf. quae adnot. Oeh.

6: 3 petitioni *AB* petitionis *Gomperz.*

4 edixerat *Gel.* ei dixerat *AB.*

7 vita panis *AB Diercks* vitae panis *Semler Reiff.* (*perperam*).

sooner and to be no longer slaves. Even if there were nothing laid down in the prayer about asking for the coming of the Kingdom, we should of our own initiative have uttered that sentiment while hastening towards the embracing of our hope.[1] The souls of the martyrs beneath the altar cry to the Lord in reproach, *How long, O Lord, dost thou not avenge our blood on the inhabitants of the earth?*[2] For indeed their vengeance is set in motion at the end of the world. Yea, let thy kingdom come, O Lord, as speedily as may be, the hope of Christians, the confounding of the gentiles, the joy of angels, that for the sake of which we suffer affliction, yea rather, that for the sake of which we pray.

6 But how gracefully has divine wisdom drawn up the order of the prayer, that after heavenly things, that is, after God's name, God's will, and God's kingdom, it should make place for petition for earthly necessities too: for the Lord had also stated the principle, *Seek ye first the kingdom and then even these things will be added to you.*[3] And yet we prefer the spiritual understanding of GIVE US TO-DAY OUR DAILY BREAD. For Christ is our bread, because Christ is life and bread is life: *I am*, he says, *the bread of life*: and a little earlier, *The bread is the word of the living God which hath come down from heaven*:[4] and again because his body is authoritatively ranked as bread—*This is my body.*[5] And so by asking for daily bread we request continuance in Christ and inseparableness from his body. But even in that this expression has a carnal acceptation, it can with all reverence be made to belong also to spiritual discipline. For it is bread he enjoins us to ask for, which thing alone is what the faithful need: for after the other things do the gentiles seek. In this sense also he enforces it by examples and rehearses it in parables when he says, *Does the Father take away the bread from his sons and hand it to the dogs?*[6] also, *When his son asks for bread, does he hand him a stone?*[7]—for he is showing what it is that sons look for from their father.

[1] Cf. Heb. 11. 13. [2] Rev. 6. 10.
[3] Matt. 6. 33; Luke 12. 31. [4] John 6. 48; cf. ibid. 33, 51.
[5] Matt. 26. 26; Mark 14. 22; Luke 22. 19; 1 Cor. 11. 24.
[6] Matt. 15. 26; Mark 7. 27. [7] Matt. 7. 9; Luke 11. 11.

a patre filii expectent. sed et nocturnus ille pulsator panem pulsabat. merito autem adiecit Da nobis hodie, ut qui praemiserat
20 Nolite de crastino cogitare quid edatis. cui rei parabolam quoque
accommodavit illius hominis qui provenientibus fructibus
ampliationem horreorum et longae securitatis spatia cogitavit,
ea ipsa nocte moritur*us*.

7 Consequens erat ut observata dei liberalitate etiam clementiam
eius precaremur: quid enim alimenta proderunt si illis reputamur
re vera quasi taurus ad victimam? sciebat dominus se solum sine
delicto esse: docet itaque petamus DIMITTI NOBIS DEBITA
5 NOSTRA. exomologesis est petitio veniae, quia qui petit veniam
delictum confitetur. sic et paenitentia demonstratur acceptabilis
deo, quia vult eam quam mortem peccatoris. debitum autem in
scripturis delicti figura est, quod perinde iudicio debeatur et ab
eo exigatur, nec evadat iustitiam exactionis nisi donetur exactio,
10 sicut illi servo dominus debitum remisit: huc enim spectat exemplum parabolae totius. nam et quod idem servus a domino
liberatus non perinde parcit debitori suo ac propterea delatus
penes dominum tortori delegatur ad solvendum novissimum
quadrantem, id est modicum usque delictum, eo competit quod
15 remittere nos quoque profitemur debitoribus nostris. iam et alibi
ex hac specie orationis, Remittite, inquit, et remittetur vobis: et
cum interrogasset Petrus si septies remittendum esset fratri, Immo,
inquit, septuagies septies, ut legem in melius reformaret, quod in
Genesi de Cain septies de Lamech autem septuagies septies ultio
20 reputata est.

8 Adiecit ad plenitudinem tam expeditae orationis, ut non de

6: 18 pulsabat *AB Diercks* poscebat Urs. *Reiff.* (*citra consuetudinem scriptoris*).
   23 ea ipsa nocte moriturus *scripsi* is ipsa nocte moritur *AB, ceteris in A*
   humore evanidis: sed redundat is, neque satis cum praecedentibus cohaeret
   clausula: moriturus *Diercks.*
7: 2 illis *AB* illi Rig. *Reiff. Diercks.*
   7 quia vult *AB Reiff. Diercks* qui mavult Leopoldus, Oeh. (*vix observato*
   stylo Septimiano).

Moreover that midnight knocker was knocking for bread.[1] Also with good reason he has added, *Give us to-day*, seeing he had already said, *Take no thought for tomorrow, what ye shall eat.*[2] And to that theme he also applied the parable of the man who, when the fruits were abundant, thought of extending his barns, and of periods of long unconcern, though he was to die that very night.[3]

7 It is with good reason that having taken note of God's generosity we also beseech his clemency. For what will food profit us if by it we are simply being accounted as a bull for the sacrifice?[4] The Lord knew that he alone was without wrong:[5] and so he teaches us to ask for OUR DEBTS TO BE FORGIVEN US. A request for pardon is a confession ⟨of wrong⟩, seeing that he who asks for pardon admits the wrong done. So also penitence is shown to be acceptable to God, because he prefers it to the death of the sinner.[6] Now debt in the scriptures is a metaphor for wrong-doing, in that wrong-doing no less owes a debt to judgement and is avenged by it, and does not escape the justice of restitution, unless restitution be remitted, as his lord forgave that servant his debt[7]—for this the example of the whole parable has in view. For the fact that the same servant, set free by his lord, does not likewise spare his debtor, and, being on that account reported before his lord, is delivered to the tormentor until the last farthing be paid (meaning the very smallest wrong), fits in with this, that we profess that WE ALSO FORGIVE OUR DEBTORS. And moreover in another place, in accordance with this clause of the prayer, he says, *Forgive and it shall be forgiven you.*[8] Also when Peter had asked whether he must forgive his brother seven times, *Yea*, he said, *seventy times seven*,[9] so as to recast the Law in better form, because in Genesis vengeance was reckoned in the case of Cain seven times, but of Lamech seventy times seven.[10]

8 For the completion of this short and convenient prayer, so that

---

[1] Luke 11. 5.   [2] Matt. 6. 34.   [3] Luke 12. 16–21.
[4] Cf. Ps. 44. 22; Rom. 8. 36.   [5] Cf. John 8. 46.
[6] Cf. Ezek. 8. 23, 32.   [7] Matt. 18. 23–36.
[8] Luke 6. 37.   [9] Matt. 18. 21.   [10] Gen. 4. 24.

remittendis tantum sed etiam de avertendis in totum delictis
supplicaremus, NE NOS INDUCAS IN TEMPTATIONEM, id est,
ne nos patiaris induci, ab eo utique qui temptat. ceterum absit
5 ut dominus temptare videatur, quasi aut ignoret fidem cuiusque
aut deicere sit *gestiens*: diaboli est et infirmitas et malitia. nam
et Abraham non temptandae fidei gratia sacrificare de filio iusserat, sed probandae, ut per eum faceret exemplum praecepto suo
quo mox praecepturus erat ne qu*i* pignora deo cariora haberet.
10 ipse a diabolo temptatus praesidem et artificem temptationis
demonstravit. hunc locum posterioribus confirmat, Orate, dicens,
ne temptemini: adeo temptati sunt, dominum deserendo quia
somno potius indulserant quam orationi. ergo respondet clausula,
interpretans quid sit Ne nos deducas in temptationem: hoc est
15 enim, SED DEVEHE NOS A MALO.

9   Compendiis pauculorum verborum quot attinguntur edicta
prophetarum evangeliorum apostolorum, sermones domini,
parabolae exempla praecepta, quot simul expunguntur officia:
dei honor in patre, fidei testimonium in nomine, oblatio obsequii
5 in voluntate, commemoratio spei in regno, petitio vitae in pane,
exomologesis debitorum in deprecatione, sollicitudo temptatio-
num in postulatione tutelae. quid mirum? deus solus docere
potuit quomodo se vellet orari: ab ipso igitur ordinata religio
orationis, et de spiritu eius iam tunc cum ex ore divino ferretur
10 animata, suo privilegio ascendit in caelum commendans patri
quae filius docuit.

10   Quoniam tamen dominus, prospector humanarum necessi-
tatum, seorsum post traditam orandi disciplinam, Petite, inquit,

8:6 gestiens *Rig.* ...stiens *A* consentiens *B.*
   9 ne qui *Reiff.* neque *AB* ne quis *Mercerus* ne quae *Oeh.* neque...habenda
     Gel. (*quem forsan sequi malis*).
9:1 *Incipit codex D: quem qui exarabat quae sequuntur capitula pro integro opere*
     videtur habuisse   pauculorum *D* paucorum *AB.*
   4 fidei *D* fides *AB.*
   8 quomodo *D* ut *AB* (*forsan recte*).

our supplication might be not only for the forgiveness but also for the total removal of wrong-doings, he added LEAD US NOT INTO TEMPTATION—that is, suffer us not to be led, of course by the one who does tempt. For God forbid that the Lord should be supposed to tempt,[1] as though he were either ignorant of each man's faith or desirous of overthrowing it. Both weakness and malice belong to the devil. For even Abraham he had commanded to make a sacrifice of his son[2] not for the sake of testing his faith but of approving it, so that by him he might set an example for his own precept by which he was afterwards to command that no man should hold his children dearer than God.[3] He himself, being tempted of the devil, showed who is the patron and artificer of temptation. This passage he confirms in the words that come later, saying, *Pray that ye be not tempted*:[4] actually they were tempted, in forsaking the Lord because they had given themselves to sleep in preference to prayer. So the conclusion ⟨of the prayer⟩ corresponds, interpreting the meaning of *Bring us not into temptation*: for this is, BUT REMOVE US FROM THE EVIL.

9 How many edicts of prophets, gospels, and apostles, how many discourses, parables, examples, and precepts of the Lord, are touched upon in the brevities of a few short words, how many duties are summed up all at once—in *Father* the honour of God, in *name* ⟨our⟩ witness to the faith, in *will* the sacrifice of obedience, in *kingdom* the commemoration of ⟨our⟩ hope, in *bread* the petition for life, in the prayer for pardon the confession of debts, in the request for safeguard wariness against temptations. And what wonder? God alone was competent to teach us how he wished to be prayed to. As therefore by him the sanctity of the prayer was ordained, as it did, at the very time when it was being brought forth of the divine lips, receive life from his Spirit, ⟨so⟩ by its own special right it ascends into heaven, commending to the Father the things the Son has taught.

10 Yet since the Lord, the foreseer of human necessities,[5] says in a different context, after the delivery of his instruction on

---

[1] Cf. Jas. 1. 13.   [2] Gen. 22. 1.   [3] Matt. 10. 37.
[4] Matt. 26. 41; Mark 14. 38; Luke 22. 46.   [5] Matt. 6. 8.

et accipietis, et sunt quae petantur pro circumstantia cuiusque, praemissa legitima et ordinaria oratione quasi fundamento, 5 accedentium ius est desideriorum superstruendi extrinsecus petitiones, cum memoria tamen praeceptorum, ne quantum a praeceptis tantum ab auribus dei longe simus.

11 Memoria praeceptorum viam orationibus sternit ad caelum: quorum praecipuum est ne prius ascendamus ad altare dei quam si quid discordiae vel offensae cum fratribus contraxerimus resolvamus. quale est enim ad pacem dei accedere sine pace, ad 5 remissionem debitorum cum retentione? quomodo placabit patrem iratus in fratrem, cum omnis ira ab initio interdicta sit nobis? nam et Ioseph dimittens fratres suos ad perducendum patrem, Et ne, inquit, irascamini in via. nos scilicet monuit (alias enim via cognominatur disciplina nostratum) ne in via 10 orationis constituti ad patrem cum ira incedamus. exinde aperte dominus amplians legem iram in fratrem homicidio superponit: ne verbo quidem malo permittit expungi. etiam si irascendum est, non ultra solis receptum, ut apostolus admonet: quam autem temerarium est aut diem sine oratione transigere dum cessas 15 fratri satisfacere, aut orationem perseverante iracundia perdere.

12 Nec ab ira solummodo sed omni omnino confusione animi libera esse debet orationis intentio, de tali spiritu emissa qualis est spiritus ad quem mittitur. neque enim agnosci poterit ⟨a⟩ spiritu sancto spiritus inquinatus, aut tristis a laeto aut impeditus a libero: 5 nemo adversarium recipit, nemo nisi comparem suum admittit.

13 Ceterum quae ratio est manibus quidem ablutis spiritu vero sordente orationem obire, quando et ipsis manibus spiritales munditiae sint necessariae, ut a falso a caede a saevitia a veneficiis

10: 5 accedentium D   accidentium AB   ius est desideriorum AB   desideriorum ius est D (*ubi si codd. AB acceperis testimonium necessario post* fundamento *virgula punges: si vero D secutus fueris haud necessario*).
    6 quantum D   quam AB (*forsan recte*).
    7 *Post* longe simus *capita diviserunt* Mur. Diercks: *ceteri post* praeceptorum.
11: 4 quale AD   quid B.
    9 alias AB   Helias D.   nostratum Diercks (*solito suo acumine*) nostra. tum ABD *edd.*
12: 1 confusione AB   contusione D.
    3 a *add.* Gel.: *probant* Pam. Rig. Mur. *om.* ABD.

prayer, *Ask and ye shall receive*,[1] and as there are things to be asked for according to each man's circumstances, we have the right, after rehearsing the prescribed and regular prayer as a foundation, to make from other sources a superstructure of petitions for additional desires: yet with mindfulness of the precepts, lest we be as far from the ears of God as we are from the precepts.

11 Mindfulness of the precepts paves for prayers the way to heaven: and the chief of them is that we go not up to the altar of God before we cancel whatever of discord or offence we have contracted with the brethren.[2] For how can one without peace draw nigh to the peace of God, or to the remission of debts with the retention of them? How shall one propitiate the Father while angry against the brother, when from the beginning onwards all anger is forbidden us?[3] For Joseph also, when sending his brethren to fetch their father, said, *And see that ye become not angry on the way.*[4] His advice was meant for us (for elsewhere our people's doctrine has the name of 'way')[5] that when in the way of prayer we should not journey towards the Father in anger. Consequently the Lord, in an evident expansion of the Law, equates anger against one's brother with homicide:[6] not even with an evil word does he suffer it to be given effect. Even if one has to be angry, not beyond sunset, as the apostle gives warning:[7] but how rash it is either to pass a day without prayer while you delay to give satisfaction to your brother, or to waste your prayer by persisting in anger.

12 And not from anger only, but from all and every perturbation of mind, ought the intensity of prayer to be free, being sent forth from such a spirit as is that Spirit to whom it is sent forth. For a defiled spirit can receive no recognition from holy Spirit— nor sad from glad, nor fettered from free. No man opens his door to an opponent, no man lets in anyone but his like.

13 Moreover what sense is there in addressing oneself to prayer with washen hands but a dirty spirit?[8]—especially as the hands themselves stand in need of spiritual cleanliness, so as to be lifted

---

[1] John 16. 24.   [2] Matt. 5. 23, 24.   [3] Matt. 5. 22.

[4] Gen. 45. 24.   [5] Acts 9. 2; 19. 9, 23.   [6] Matt. 5. 22, 23.

[7] Eph. 4. 26.   [8] Matt. 15. 1–20; Mark 7. 1–23.

ab idololatria ceterisque maculis quae spiritu conceptae manuum
5 opera transiguntur purae alleventur ? hae sunt verae munditiae, non
quas plerique superstitiose curant, ad omnem orationem, etiam
cum a lavacro totius corporis veniunt, aquam sumentes. id cum
scrupulosius percontarer et rationem requirerem, comperi commemorationem esse Pilati: manus abluisse in domini deditione.
10 nos dominum adoramus, non dedimus: immo et adversari
debemus deditoris exemplo nec propterea manus abluere, nisi
ob aliquod conversationis humanae inquinamentum conscientiae
causa lavemus. ceterum satis mundae sunt manus quas toto cum
corpore in Christo semel lavimus.

14 Omnibus licet membris lavet quotidie Israel, nunquam tamen
mundus est. certe manus eius semper immundae, sanguine prophetarum et ipsius domini incrustatae in aeternum: et ideo conscientia patrum haereditarii rei nec attollere eas ad dominum
5 audent, ne exclamet aliquis Esaias, ne exhorreat Christus. nos
vero non attollimus tantum sed etiam expandimus, et dominica
passione modulantes, et orantes confitemur Christo.

15 Sed quoniam unum aliquod attigimus vacuae observationis,
non pigebit cetera quoque denotare quibus merito vanitas expro-
branda est, siquidem sine ullius aut dominici aut apostolici praecepti auctoritate fiunt. huiusmodi enim non religioni sed super-
5 stitioni deputantur, affectata et coacta et curiosi potius quam
rationalis officii, certe vel eo coercenda quod gentilibus adaequent,
ut est quorundam expositis paenulis orationem facere: sic enim
adeunt ad idola nationes. quod utique, si fieri oporteret, apostoli

13: 5 opera *AB* opere *D*.
    7 a lavacro *D* lavacro *AB*   aquam *AB* ad aquam *D* (*qui tamen retinet* sumentes).
    9 Pilati: manus abluisse *ita pungebam* pilati manus abluisse *D*: *om. AB* Pilatum manus abluisse *Reiff*. Pilati: eum manus abluisse *Diercks*. deditione *D* dedicationem *AB* (*manifesto errore*).
    12 *totum locum ita pungebam*: ob aliquod *D* quod *AB*
    13 lavemus *B* ['*Reiff. falso scribit in AB deesse*': *ita Diercks, qui tamen in textum non admisit*] *om. AD*
14: 3 incrustatae *D Reiff. Diercks* cruentatae *AB Oeh*.
    6–7 dominica passione modulantes *scripsi* dominica passione *ABD* modulantes *B* modulatum *AD* modulati *Oeh*. dominica passione modulata *Diercks*.
15: 8 si *om. D*   apostoli qui *D* apostoliq: *A* apostoli quae *B*.

up pure of fraud, murder, violence, sorcery, idolatry, and the other defilements which, conceived in the spirit, are brought to effect by the agency of the hands. This is the true cleanliness, not that which certain persons are superstitiously careful of, rinsing their hands at every prayer, even when they have just come from a bath of the whole body. When I asked rather searching questions, and demanded the reason, I found it to be a recollection of Pilate, ⟨because⟩ he rinsed his hands on delivering up the Lord.[1] We worship the Lord, we do not deliver him up: in fact we ought to set ourselves against the example of the man who delivered him up, and for that reason not rinse our hands, unless we wash them for some defilement of human conversation for conscience' sake. For the rest, hands are clean enough which, along with the whole body, we have once for all washed in Christ.

14 Though Israel wash every day, in all his members, yet is he never clean.[2] His hands at all events are always unclean, crusted over for ever with the blood of the prophets and of the Lord himself: and therefore being, through consciousness of their fathers' guilt, criminals by inheritance,[3] they dare not lift them up to the Lord, lest some Isaiah cry out,[4] lest Christ be horrified. We however not only lift them up,[5] but also spread them out, and, modulating them by the Lord's passion, in our prayers also express our faith in Christ.

15 But since we have touched upon one matter of empty observation, we shall not count it irksome to censure the rest of the practices which may with good reason be stigmatized as vain, seeing that the doing of them has the authority of no precept of the Lord or of the apostles. For things of this kind are reckoned not to religion but to superstition, matters of affectation and constraint, of officious rather than reasonable service,[6] and certainly to be suppressed (if for no other reason) because they put us on a level with the gentiles—as it is the practice of some to pray with their coats off, for so do the nations approach their idols. But surely if this were a right thing to do, the apostles, who give instruction concerning demeanour during prayer, would have

[1] Matt. 27. 24.   [2] Isa. 1. 15, 16.   [3] Matt. 23. 31; Acts 7. 51, 52.
[4] Isa. 1. 15.   [5] 1 Tim. 2. 8.   [6] Rom. 12. 1.

qui de habitu orandi docent comprehendissent—nisi si qui putant
10 Paulum paenulam suam in oratione penes Carpum reliquisse.
deus scilicet non audiat paenulatos, qui tres sanctos in fornace
Babylonii regis orantes cum sarabaris et tiaris suis exaudivit.

16 Item quod assignata oratione assidendi mos est quibusdam,
non perspicio rationem nisi quam pueri volunt. quid enim? si
Hermas ille, cuius scriptura fere Pastor inscribitur, transacta
oratione non super lectum assedisset verum aliud quid fecisset, id
5 quoque ad observationem vindicaremus? utique non. simpliciter
enim et nunc positum est, Cum adorassem et assedissem super
lectum, ad ordinem narrationis non ad instar disciplinae. alioquin
nusquam erit adorandum nisi ubi fuerit lectus: immo contra
scripturam fecerit siquis in cathedra aut subsellio sederit. porro
10 cum perinde faciant nationes [vel] adoratis sigillaribus suis
residendo, vel propterea in nobis reprehendi meretur quod apud
idola celebratur. eo apponitur et inreverentiae crimen etiam ipsis
nationibus si quid saperent intellegendum. si quidem inreverens
est assidere sub conspectu contraque conspectum eius quem cum
15 maxime reverearis et venereris, quanto magis sub conspectu dei
vivi, angelo adhuc orationis adstante, factum istud inreligiosissi-
mum est?—nisi exprobramus deo quod nos oratio fatigaverit.

17 Atqui cum modestia et humilitate adorantes magis commendabimus deo preces nostras, ne ipsis quidem manibus sublimius
elatis sed temperate ac probe elevatis, ne vultu quidem in audaciam
erecto. nam et ille publicanus, qui non tantum prece sed et vultu
5 humiliatus atque deiectus orabat, iustificatior pharisaeo procacis-
simo discessit. sonos etiam vocis subiectos esse oportet: aut

15: 12 sarabaris *Gel.* sabaris *ABD.*

16: 2 quam pueri volunt. quid enim? *om. AB.*

   10 perinde *AB* proinde *D.*   vel adoratis *ABD* vel *om. Gel.*

   14 cum maxime *B* quam maxime *A* maxime *D.*

17: 1 commendabimus *Oeh.* commendavimus *AD* commendamus *B.*

    3 elevatis *scripsi* elatis *libri et edd. utraque vice, nisi quod priori vice deletum vult Jun.*

    4 et *om. D.*   6 sonos *AB* sono *D.*   esse *om. AD.*

included it—unless any think that Paul left his coat behind with
Carpus during prayer.[1] God, I suppose, would not hear men with
their coats on: though he did hear and answer the three saints in
the Babylonian king's furnace, when they prayed in their hosen
and their hats.[2]

16 Also, that some have a custom of sitting down at the sealing
of the prayer, I do not clearly see the reason, except one which
children approve of. For consider: if that Hermas, whose writing
is entitled *The Shepherd* or something of the sort, had not sat
down upon his bed when he had finished his prayer, but had done
you know what, should we claim that that also must be made an
observance? Surely not. For even as it is it is stated without any
afterthought, *When I had prayed and had sat down on the bed,*[3] for
the order of the narrative, not with the import of an instruction.
Otherwise one will have to pray nowhere except where there is
a bed: in fact anyone will act contrary to scripture who sits in the
chair or on the bench. Moreover, since the gentiles do likewise,
sitting down after worshipping their puppets, for that reason
alone a practice calls for reproof among us which is used in the
presence of idols. Added to that is the charge of disrespect besides, which even the gentiles might understand if they had any
feeling. If in fact it is disrespectful to sit down in the presence
and in spite of the presence of one whom you highly respect and
esteem, how much more is this act most irreligious in the presence
of the living God, while the angel of prayer is still standing
by[4]—unless we are remonstrating with God because the prayer has
made us tired.

17 Moreover we shall the rather commend our prayers to God
by worshipping with restraint and humility, not even lifting the
hands too high but raising them temperately and meetly, not even
holding up our eyes in presumption. For that Publican, who
prayed with humility and dejection not of prayer only but of
countenance, went away justified rather than the insolent
Pharisee.[5] Even the tones of our voice need to be subdued—or

---

[1] 2 Tim. 4. 13.   [2] Dan. 3. 21.
[3] Herm. *Vis.* 5.
[4] Cf. Tobit 12. 12; Luke 1. 11; Rev. 8. 3, 4.   [5] Luke 18. 14.

quantis arteriis opus est si pro sono audiamur? deus autem non
vocis sed cordis auditor est, sicut conspector. daemonium oraculi
Pythii, Et mutum, inquit, intellego et non loquentem exaudio:
10 dei aures sonum expectant? quomodo ergo oratio Ionae de imo
ventre ceti per tantae bestiae viscera ab ipsis abyssis per tantam
aequoris molem ad caelum potuit evadere? quid amplius referent
isti qui clarius adorant, nisi quod proximis obstrepunt? immo
prodendo petitiones suas quid minus faciunt quam si in publico
15 orent?

18 Alia iam consuetudo invaluit: ieiunantes habita oratione cum
fratribus subtrahunt osculum pacis quod est signaculum orationis.
quando autem magis conferenda cum fratribus pax est nisi cum
oratio ⟨operatio⟩ne commendabilior ascendit, ut ipsi de nostra
5 operatione participent qui maduerint, de sua pace fratri trans-
ferendo? quae oratio cum divortio sancti osculi integra? quem
domino officium facientem impedit pax? quale sacrificium est
a quo sine pace disceditur? quaecumque ratio sit, non erit potior
praecepti observatione quo iubemur ieiunia nostra celare: iam
10 enim de abstinentia osculi agnoscimur ieiunantes. sed et si qua
ratio est, ne tamen huic praecepto reus sis, potes domi, si forte,
inter quos latere ieiunium in totum non datur, differre pacem:
ubicumque autem alibi operationem tuam abscondere potes, debes
meminisse praecepti. ita et disciplinae *foris* et consuetudini domi
15 satisfacies. sic et die paschae, quo communis et quasi publica
ieiunii religio est, merito deponimus osculum, nihil curantes de
occultando quod cum omnibus faciamus.

17: 10 imo *om. AB.*

  15 *Post* in publico orent *in margine cod.* D *leguntur,* veraciter namque orare
    est amaros in compunctione gemitus et incomposita verba resonare.
    Nota g̃g̃ in moral. libro.

18: 3 cum oratio operatione *Diercks* cum oratione *AB* cum operationis cum
    oratio *D* cum oratio *Rig.*: *alia alii tentaverunt.*

  5 qui maduerint *scripsi* qua maduerint *D Reiff.* quam auderent *AB* qui
    eam adiuverint *Diercks* transferendo *scripsi* (*nec tamen multum mihi
    adridet*) transigent *D* transigendus *A* transigendo *Oeh. Reiff.* (*quod
    quid sibi velit haud intellego*).

  8 disceditur *D* receditur *AB* ratio *D* oratio *AB* (*manifesto errore*).

  11 praecepto reus sis *D* praeceptore ussis *A* praeceptor tu sis *B.*

  14 foris *Gel.* iuris *ABD.*

  17 occultando *D* oscultando *A* osculando *B.*

else what lungs are called for if we are heard in proportion to the noise. But God is a hearer, as he is a discerner, not of the voice but of the heart.[1] The demon of the Pythian oracle says, *Dumb do I understand him, and while he speaks not I hearken*: do God's ears wait for a noise? How then had Jonah's prayer power to climb up to heaven from the bottom of the belly of the whale through the entrails of that great monster, from the very depths through all that mass of waters?[2] What profit will these win who are praying too articulately, except that they are shouting down the people next them? Nay but, by divulging their own petitions what less are they doing than if they were praying at street corners?[3]

18 Still another custom has become prevalent: when they are keeping a fast, after joining in the prayer along with the brethren, they withhold the kiss of peace, which is the seal of the prayer. But what better time is there for peace to be exchanged with the brethren, than when the prayer has ascended with the additional commendation of the good work, so that those also who have broken their fast may partake of the benefit of our good work by transferring a share of their own peace to the brother ⟨who remains fasting⟩? What prayer is unmutilated when divorced from the holy kiss? Whom does the peace hinder in the performance of his duty to the Lord? What sort of sacrifice is that from which one retires without the peace? Whatever the reason may be, it cannot be more important than the observance of the precept by which we are commanded to conceal our fasts:[4] for it is at once evident that we are fasting, if we abstain from the kiss. Moreover even if there is some reason, you can (for the sake of not transgressing this precept) defer the peace at home, it may be, among those who cannot be wholly ignorant of your fast: but anywhere else, where you are in a position to hide your good work, your duty is to keep in mind the precept. By this means you will do justice to the rules in public and to the custom at home. Thus also on the day of the Passover, on which there is a general and as it were official obligation of fasting, we rightly omit the kiss, taking no heed to keep hidden a thing we are doing in the company of all.

---

[1] Heb. 4. 12. [2] Jonah 2.
[3] Matt. 6. 5. [4] Matt. 6. 16–18.

19 Similiter et de stationum diebus: non putant plerique sacrificiorum orationibus interveniendum, quod statio solvenda sit accepto corpore domini. ergo devotum deo obsequium eucharistia resolvit? an magis deo obligat? nonne sollemnior erit statio
5 tua si et ad aram dei steteris? accepto corpore domini et reservato utrumque salvum est, et participatio sacrificii et exsecutio officii. si statio de militari exemplo nomen accepit (nam et militia dei sumus) utique nulla laetitia sive tristitia obveniens castris stationes militum rescindit: nam laetitia libentius, tristitia sollicitius,
10 administrabit disciplinam.

20 De habitu vero dumtaxat feminarum varietas observationis effecit post sanctissimum apostolum nos vel maxime nullius loci homines impudenter retractare, nisi quod non impudenter si secundum apostolum retractemus. de modestia quidem cultus
5 et ornatus aperta praescriptio est etiam Petri, cohibentis eodem ore quia eodem et spiritu quo Paulus et vestium gloriam et auri superbiam et crinium lenonem operositatem.

21 Sed, quod promisce observatur per ecclesias, quasi incertum, id retractandum est, velarine debeant virgines annon. qui enim virginibus indulgent capitis immunitatem hoc niti videntur quod apostolus non virgines nominatim sed mulieres designaverit
5 velandas esse, nec sexum ut diceret feminas, sed gradum sexus dicendo mulieres: nam si sexum nominasset feminas dicendo, absolute definisset de omni muliere: at cum unum gradum sexus nominat, alium tacendo secernit. potuit enim, inquiunt, aut et virgines nominare specialiter aut compendio generaliter feminas.

19: 1 diebus: *ita pungebam.*
    7 accepit *D*   accipit *AB.*
    10 *post* disciplinam *deficit B.*
20: 2 effecit *D*   efficit *A.*
    6 ore *Rig.* more *AD.*   quo Paulus *om. A.*
    7 crinium *A* criminum *D.*   operositatem *A* morositatem *D.*
21: 1 *In cod. A post* ecclesias quas, *nullo lacunae signo adhibito, statim sequitur de cult. fem.* i. 5 disposita utensilitas.

19 Similarly also concerning the station days: a number of people think they ought not to participate in the prayers of the sacrifices, because the station, they allege, has to be broken by the reception of the Lord's body. Does then the Eucharist cancel a devout service to God? or does it rather bind us closer to God? Will not your station be more ceremonious if you have also stood at God's altar? By your accepting the Lord's body and reserving it both things are safe, your partaking of the sacrifice and your performance of your duty. If 'station' has received its name from military precedent (for we are also God's militia),[1] evidently neither joy nor sorrow occurring to a camp releases the soldiers from guard-duty: for joy will administer discipline with a better will, sorrow with greater concern.

20 But on the subject of clothing, that of females at least, the variety of usage has caused me, a man of especially little standing, presumptuously, after the holy apostle,[2] to write a treatise—except that there is no presumption if my treatment is in keeping with the apostle. In fact concerning moderation of toilet and adornment there is the evident authority also of Peter, who with the same voice, because with the same Spirit, as Paul, restrains both the vain glory of apparel and the pride of gold and the seductive elaboration of the hair.[3]

21 But an observance which is general throughout the churches —as though it were uncertain, discussion of it is necessary—whether virgins are bound to wear the veil or not. Those who grant virgins immunity of head seem to take their stand on the fact that the apostle has signified not that virgins specifically but that women must wear the veil[4]—not the sex, so as to say 'females', but the rank of the sex, saying 'women'. For if he had specified the sex by saying 'females', he would have been laying down a general rule concerning any and every woman; but when he specifies one rank of the sex he excludes the other by abstaining from mentioning it. For it was possible, they say, for him either to have mentioned virgins also specifically, or briefly in generic terms 'females'.

---

[1] 2 Tim. 2. 3.   [2] 1 Cor. 11. 3–16.
[3] 1 Pet. 3. 1–6.   [4] 1 Cor. 11. 3–16.

22 Qui ita concedunt recogitare debent de statu vocabuli ipsius: quid est mulier a primis quidem literis sanctorum commentariorum? Nam invenient sexus esse nomen, non gradum sexus: siquidem Evam nondum virum expertam deus mulierem
5 et feminam cognominavit[, feminam qua sexus generaliter, mulierem qua gradus sexus specialiter]. ita quo iam tunc innupta adhuc Eva mulieris vocabulo fuit, commune id vocabulum et virgini factum est. nec mirum si apostolus, eodem utique spiritu actus quo cum omnis scriptura divina tum et illa Genesis digesta
10 est, eadem voce usus est mulierem ponendo quae exemplo Evae innuptae et virgini competat. cetera denique consonant. nam et hoc ipso quod virgines non nominavit sicut alio in loco ubi de nubendo docet, satis praedicat de omni muliere et de toto sexu dictum nec distinctum esse inter⟨mulierem et⟩ virginem ⟨quam⟩
15 omnino non nominat. qui enim alibi distinguere meminit ubi scilicet differentia postulat (distinguit autem utramque speciem suis vocabulis designans) ubi non distinguit, dum utramque non nominat nullam vult differentiam intellegi. quid quod Graeco sermone quo literas apostolus fecit usui est mulieres vocare quam
20 feminas, id est γυναῖκας quam θηλείας? igitur si pro sexus nomine vocabulum istud frequentatur quod est interpretatione pro eo quod est femina, sexum nominavit dicens γυναῖκα: in sexu autem et virgo contingitur. sed et manifesta pronuntiatio est: Omnis, inquit, mulier adorans et prophetans intecto capite dedecorat
25 caput suum. quid est 'omnis mulier', nisi omnis aetatis omnis ordinis omnis condicionis? nihil mulieris excepit dicendo 'omnis', sicut nec viri non velandi: proinde enim Omnis vir, inquit. sicut ergo in masculino sexu sub viri nomine etiam investis velari

---

22: 1 concedunt D   contendunt x: sed cf. quod supra scriptum est § 21 indulgent.
3 invenient x Routh alii   inveniunt D.
5 feminam...specialiter secl. Diercks.
6 ita quo iam scribebam   forsan postea secludendum mulieris   ita quoniam Oeh.   itaque iam D.   9 divina tum x   divinitatum D.
11 consonant x   ñ. sonant D.   14 mulierem et...quam add. x.
23 contingitur D edd.: quaeritur an scribendum continetur, collato quod infra scriptum est tenentur.
26 conditionis D.
27 viri non scripsi: alioquin quid hoc loco facias nescio   vir nec D.
28 velari vetatur Mur.   velare vertatur D.

22 Those who grant this concession are bound to reconsider the quality of the term in question—what is 'woman' from the very first pages of the sacred records? They will find it is the name of the sex, not a rank of the sex, inasmuch as before Eve had knowledge of her husband God named her 'woman' and 'female'.[1]...Thus the term 'woman', by which Eve, while still unwedded, was already ⟨described⟩, that term was made common also to the virgin. And no wonder if the apostle, led as he was by the same Spirit by which, like the whole of divine scripture, so also that ⟨book of⟩ Genesis was compiled, has used the same expression, writing 'woman',[2] so that, by the precedent of Eve who was unwedded, it should apply also to the virgin. Further ⟨considerations⟩ are indeed to the same effect. For by the very fact of his not specifying virgins, as he has done in another place where he is teaching about ⟨their⟩ marrying,[3] he makes it clear enough that the statement refers to every woman and the whole sex, and that no distinction is made between 'woman' and the virgin whom he altogether abstains from specifying. For one who in another place, where in fact the difference demands it, remembers to make the distinction (for he does make a distinction, designating both species under their proper terms), in places where he makes no distinction wishes no difference to be understood, seeing he does not specify them both. Also, in the Greek language, in which the apostle wrote, it is more usual to call them 'women' than 'females', that is, *gynaîkes* than *theleîai*. As therefore for the name of the sex that term is in common use which is by interpretation equivalent to 'female', he specified the sex when he said *gyné*: and in the sex the virgin also is alluded to. Moreover his pronouncement is clear: *Every woman*, he says, *praying or prophesying with her head uncovered is dishonouring her head.*[4] What is 'every woman' if not 'of every age, of every rank, of every condition'? When he says 'every' he includes the whole of ⟨the class⟩ 'woman'—so too of 'man' who must not have his head covered: for to the same effect he says 'every man'.[5] As then in the male sex, under the designation 'man', even the young boy

[1] Gen. 1. 27; 2. 23.   [2] 1 Cor. 11. 5.
[3] 1 Cor. 7. 25.   [4] 1 Cor. 11. 6.   [5] 1 Cor. 11. 4.

vetatur, ita et in feminino sub nomine mulieris etiam virgo
30 velari iubetur. aequaliter in utroque sexu minor aetas maioris
sequatur disciplinam, aut velentur et virgines masculi si non
velantur et virgines feminae, quia nec isti nominatim tenentur:
aliud sit vir *et* investis si aliud est mulier et virgo. 'nempe propter
angelos ait velari oportere, quod angeli propter filias hominum
35 desciverunt a deo.' quis ergo contendat solas mulieres, id est
nuptas iam et virginitatem defunctas, concupiscentiae ⟨esse⟩, nisi
si non licet et virgines specie praestare et amatores invenire? immo
videamus ne virgines solas concupierint, cum dicat scriptura
Filias hominum, quia potuit uxores hominum nominasse vel
40 feminas indifferenter. etiam quod ait, Et acceperunt sibi in uxores,
eo facit, quod accipiuntur in uxores quae vacant scilicet: de non
vacantibus autem aliter enuntiasset. itaque vacant tam viduitate
quam et virginitate. adeo sexum nominando generaliter filias, et
species in genere commiscuit. item cum dicit naturam ipsam
45 docere velandum feminis esse, quae capillum pro tegumento et
ornamento mulieribus assignarit, nonne idem tegumentum et
idem honor capitis virginibus quoque adscriptus est? si mulieri
turpe est radi, et virgini proinde. in quibus ergo una condicio
capitis deputatur, una et disciplina capitis exigitur, etiam ad eas
50 virgines quas pueritia defendit: a primo enim femina nominata
est. sic denique et Israel observat. sed si non observaret, nostra
lex ampliata atque suppleta defenderet sibi adiectionem, virginibus
quoque iniciens velamentum. excusetur nunc aetas quae sexum
suum ignorat, simplicitatis privilegium teneat: nam et Eva et

22: 33 et *add. Mur.*

    36 virginitatem D *sec. scriptoris nostri consuetudinem* virginitate *Oeh.* esse
addendum putabam: ita et Reiff.

    38 videamus ne *Oeh.* videmus ne D videmus quod *Mur. Routh.*

    43 sexum *deletum voluit Diercks.*

    48 proinde D perinde *Mur. Reiff.*

    52–4 *ita pungebam Diercksium aliquatenus secutus.*

is forbidden to be covered, so in the female sex under the designation 'woman' even the virgin is commanded to be veiled. Equally in either sex let the lower age follow the rule imposed on the higher: or else let male virgins be covered if female virgins are not covered, since neither are these specifically ⟨said to be⟩ under obligation: let the boy be something different from the man, if the virgin is something different from the woman. You object that he says they ought to be veiled because of the angels,[1] because the angels revolted from God for the sake of the daughters of men.[2] Will anyone then claim that only women, that is married ones who have now outlived their virginity, are an object of concupiscence—unless perchance it is impossible for virgins to be exceeding fair and to find admirers? Rather let us consider whether it was not virgins alone that they lusted after, since the scripture says 'the daughters of men': for it could have specified 'the wives of men', or even 'females' without distinction. Also the statement, *And they took them as wives for themselves,* agrees with this, because those of course are taken for wives who are free to marry: concerning such as were not free it would have used a different expression. Now women are free either by widowhood or by virginity: and thus, by calling the sex in general terms 'daughters', it has combined the species under the genus. Also when he says that nature itself teaches that females ought to use the veil,[3] by having assigned to women their hair for a covering and an adornment, is not the same covering and the same decoration of the head attributed to virgins as well? If it is shameful for a woman to be shaven,[4] no less so is it for a virgin. In the case of those therefore who are accounted of one and the same condition as regards their head, one and the same discipline of the head is demanded—not stopping short even of those virgins whom childhood makes immune: for from the first she has the name of female. Further, this also is Israel's practice. But even if it were not, our law, being expanded and supplemented, might, when it puts the veil upon virgins as well, maintain its right to make ⟨this⟩ addition. Though, as things are, the age which is ignorant of its own sex should be excused, let it have this as the privilege

[1] 1 Cor. 11. 10.   [2] Gen. 6. 2.   [3] 1 Cor. 11. 14.   [4] 1 Cor. 11. 6.

55 Adam, ubi eis contigit sapere, texerunt statim quod agnoverant. certe in quibus iam pueritia mutavit, sicut naturae ita et disciplinae debet aetas esse munifica: nam et membris et officiis mulieribus resignantur. nulla virgo est ex quo potest nubere, quoniam aetas iam in ea nupsit suo viro, id est tempori. 'sed aliqua se deo 60 vovit.' tamen et crinem exinde transfigurat et omnem habitum ad mulieris convertit. totum ergo asseveret et totum virginis praestet: quod propter deum abscondit plene obumbret. interest nostra quod dei gratia exerceat solius dei conscientiae commendare, ne quod a deo speramus ab homine compensemus. quid denudas 65 ante deum quod ante homines tegis? verecundior eris in publico quam in ecclesia? si dei gratia est et accepisti, Quid gloriaris, inquit, quasi non acceperis? quid alias ostensione tui iudicas? an alias gloria tua ad bonum invitas? atqui et ipsa periclitaris amittere, si gloriaris, et alias ad eadem pericula cogis. facile eliditur quod 70 affectione gloriae assumitur. velare, virgo, si virgo es: debes enim erubescere. si virgo es, plures oculos pati noli: nemo miretur in tuam faciem, nemo mendacium tuum sentiat. bene mentiris nuptam si caput veles: immo mentiri non videris, nupsisti enim Christo. illi carnem tuam tradidisti: age pro mariti tui disciplina: 75 si nuptas alienas velari iubet, suas utique multo magis. 'sed non

22: 61 virginis D edd.: *quaero an scribendum* mulieris.
62 plene D (*ut videtur*) Reiff. plane *Mur. Oeh.*
63 exerceat D exerceamus x exerceatur *Reiff.*
67 ostentatione *Mur.* (*praeter necessitatem*).
68 amittere…eadem pericula *Mur.* admittere…eidem periculis D.
69 eliditur *Routh* eligitur D *Mur.*

of innocency: for both Eve and Adam, when knowledge came their way, at once covered that which they had become aware of.[1] Certainly in those in whom childhood has now passed away, as their years involve the functions of nature, so ought they to involve those of discipline: for both in body and in obligations they are carried forward to women. None is a virgin from the time she is capable of marriage, for in her her years have already married their own husband, namely time. 'But such and such a one has vowed herself to God.' Yet from that time on she both alters the style of her hair and changes her whole attire to a woman's. Let her then claim to be, and display herself as, in every respect a virgin:[2] that which for God's sake she keeps hidden, let her keep fully in the shade. It is to our advantage to commend to the cognizance of God alone that which God's grace performs, lest we receive from man the recompense we hope for from God.[3] Why do you expose in the presence of God that which you keep hidden in the presence of men? Are you to be more modest in the street than in church? If it is the grace of God, and you have received it, *Why*, he says, *dost thou glory as though thou hadst not received it?*[4] Why do you pass judgement on other women by the displaying of yourself? Is it that by your glorying you are inviting other women to that which is good? Nay rather, you yourself run the danger of losing it if you glory ⟨in it⟩, and you drive others towards the same perils. That which is taken up through affectation of glory is easily stricken down. Wear the veil, O virgin, since you are a virgin: it is your duty to be shamefaced. Since you are a virgin, avoid the glances of many eyes: let no one gaze at your face: let no one be aware of your pretence. It is a good pretence of being married, if you veil your head: nay rather, it appears that it is no pretence, for you are married—to Christ.[5] To him you have surrendered your body: act according to your husband's instruction: if he commands other men's brides to be veiled, surely much more his own. 'But each single

---

[1] Gen. 3. 7.

[2] The manuscript and the editors read 'virgin': but it seems more likely that 'woman' is the correct reading.

[3] Cf. Matt. 6. 2, 5, 16.   [4] 1 Cor. 4. 7.   [5] Cf. 2 Cor. 11. 2.

putat institutionem unusquisque antecessoris commovendam.'
multi alienae consuetudini prudentiam suam et constantiam eius
addicunt. ne compellantur velari, certe voluntarias prohiberi
non oportet quae se etiam virgines negare non possunt, contentae
80 abuti in fama sua conscientiae apud deum securitate. de illis tamen
quae sponsis dicantur, constanter super meum modulum pro-
nuntiare contestarique possum velandas ex ea die esse qua ad
primum viri corpus osculo et dextera expaverint: omnia enim in
his praenupserunt, et aetas per maturitatem et caro per aetatem et
85 spiritus per conscientiam et pudor per osculi experimentum et spes
per exspectationem et mens per voluntatem. satisque nobis
exemplo Rebecca est, quae sponso demonstrato tantum, notitia
eius nubendo, velata est.

23   De genu quoque ponendo varietatem observationis patitur
oratio per pauculos quosdam qui sabbato abstinent genibus. quae
dissensio cum maxime apud ecclesias causam dicit, dominus dabit
gratiam suam ut aut cedant aut sine aliorum scandalo sententia
5 sua utantur. nos vero, sicut accepimus, solo die dominicae re-
surrectionis non ab isto tantum sed omni anxietatis habitu et
officio cavere debemus, differentes etiam negotia ne quem diabolo
locum demus. tantundem et spatio pentecostes, quae eadem
exultationis sollemnitate dispung*itur*. ceterum omni die quis
10 dubitet prosternere se deo vel prima saltem oratione qua lucem
ingredimur? ieiuniis autem et stationibus nulla oratio sine genu
et reliquo humilitatis more celebranda est: non enim oramus
tantum sed et deprecamur et satisfacimus deo domino nostro.

22: 79 contentae *Mur.*   contenti *D.*   *Totum locum ita pungebam.*
  87 demonstrato *Mur.*   demonstratum *D*   notitia *D*   notitiae *Reiff.*
  (*perperam*).
23: 7 officio *x*   officia *D.*
  8 quae *D*   quod *Oeh.*   quo *x.*
  9 sollemnitate dispungitur *Routh*   sollemnitatem dispungimur *D*: *alii alia*
  tentaverunt.

⟨bishop⟩ thinks the practice instituted by his predecessor ought not to be disturbed.' Many there are who enslave to other men's customs their own prudence and its steadfastness. Certainly it would not be right, to avoid their being compelled to wear the veil, to forbid those to take vows who are not in a position to deny that they are virgins, being content, whatever their repute may be, to stand entirely on the confidence of their conscience in the sight of God. But with regard to those who are betrothed to husbands, I am in a position firmly, beyond the range of my insignificance, to declare and attest that they must be veiled from the day on which they first bashfully experience a man's contact by kiss and hand-clasp: for in these everything is already married—their years through maturity, their body through their years, their spirit through conscience, their modesty through the experience of the kiss, their hope through expectation, their mind through consent. And Rebecca is a good enough example for us, for she, on her future husband being no more than pointed out to her, put her veil on as being married ⟨to him⟩ by ⟨merely⟩ knowing who he was.[1]

23 Also in the matter of bending the knee the prayer experiences variety of observance by ⟨the action of⟩ a certain few who on Saturday abstain from kneeling. As this dissension is even now on trial before the churches, the Lord will give his grace, that they may either yield, or else establish their judgement without offence to others. We however, as we have received ⟨the custom⟩, on the day of the Lord's resurrection alone have the duty of abstaining not only from that but from every attitude and practice of solicitude, even putting off business so as to give no place to the devil. The like also in the period of Pentecost, ⟨a festival⟩ distinguished by the same established order of exultation. But on ordinary days who would hesitate to prostrate himself to God, at least at the first prayer with which we enter on daylight? On fasts moreover, and stations, no prayer is to be performed without kneeling and the rest of the attitudes of humility: for ⟨then⟩ we do not only pray, but also make supplication and satisfaction to God our Lord.

[1] Gen. 24. 65.

24 De temporibus orationis nihil omnino praescriptum est, nisi plane omni in tempore et loco orare. sed quomodo omni loco, cum prohibemur in publico? Omni, inquit, loco quem opportunitas aut etiam necessitas importarit. neque enim contra praecep-
5 tum reputatur ab apostolis factum qui in carcere audientibus custodiis orabant et canebant deo, *aut a* Paulo qui in navi coram omnibus eucharistiam fecit.

25 De tempore vero non erit otiosa extrinsecus observatio etiam horarum quarundam, istarum dico communium quae diei interspatia signant, tertia sexta nona, quas sollemniores in scripturis invenire est. primus spiritus sanctus congregatis discipulis hora
5 tertia infusus est. Petrus, qua die visionem communitatis omnis in illo vasculo expertus est, sexta hora orandi gratia ascenderat in superiora. idem cum Ioanne ad nonam in templum adibat, ubi paralyticum sanitati reformavit. *quae* etsi simpliciter se habent *sine* ullius observationis praecepto, bonum tamen *sit* aliquam
10 constituere praesumptionem qua*e* et orandi admonitionem constringat et quasi lege ad tale munus extorqueat a negotiis interdum, ut, quod Danieli quoque legimus observatum utique ex Israelis disciplina, ne minus ter die saltem adoremus, debitores trium, patris et filii et spiritus sancti: exceptis utique legitimis orationibus
15 quae sine ulla admonitione debentur ingressu lucis et noctis. sed et cibum non prius sumere et lavacrum non prius adire quam interposita oratione fideles decet: priora enim habenda sunt spiritus refrigeria et pabula quam carnis, quia priora caelestia quam terrena.

26 Fratrem domum tuam introgressum ne sine oratione dimiseris—Vidisti, inquit, fratrem, vidisti dominum tuum—maxime

---

24: 1 De temporibus *initium* § 24 *voluit esse Diercks.*
  6 aut a Paulo *Mur.* apud Paulum *D.*
25: 1 *Inter* erit *et* otiosa *lacunam quasi iv litterarum adhibet D, ubi si velis inseras* nobis *vel* credo.
  8 quae etsi *x* suae. etsi *D.*
  9 sine...sit *Mur.* si...si *D.*
  10 quae *Routh* qua *D.*
  13 trium *om. Mur.*
  18 quia *D* et *Mur.* Oeh. (*perperam*).

24 Concerning the times of prayer no rules at all have been laid down, except of course to pray at every time and place.[1] Yet how 'at every place', when we are forbidden to pray at street corners?[2] *In every place*, he means, which propriety or even necessity suggests. For that is not accounted contrary to the precept which was done by the apostles who prayed and sang to God in prison in the hearing of the guards,[3] or by Paul who in the ship made eucharist in the presence of all.[4]

25 But concerning time, we shall not find superfluous the observance from extraneous sources of certain hours also— I mean those common ones which mark the periods of the day, the third, sixth, and ninth, which you may find in the Scriptures were in established use. The first ⟨gift of the⟩ Holy Spirit was poured out upon the assembled disciples at the third hour.[5] On the day on which Peter experienced the vision of everything common in that vessel it was at the sixth hour that he had gone to the housetop to pray.[6] He also, along with John, was going up to the Temple at the ninth hour when he restored the palsied man to soundness.[7] And although these are simple statements, without any precept of observance, yet let this be good enough to set up a sort of presumption such as may both enforce a behest to pray and may as it were by a law drag us from business for a space for such an occupation, so that (as we read also was the practice of Daniel,[8] arising evidently from Israel's discipline) we may worship not less than at least thrice a day, being the debtors of three, the Father, the Son, and the Holy Spirit, in addition of course to our statutory prayers which without any behest are due at the coming in of daylight and night. Also it is seemly for the faithful not to take food or go to the bath without first interposing a prayer: for the refreshment and sustenance of the spirit ought to be given precedence over those of the flesh, because heavenly things have precedence over earthly.

26 Let not a brother who has entered your house depart without a prayer (*You have seen a brother*, it says, *you have seen your Lord*),

---

[1] Eph. 6. 18; 1 Tim. 2. 8.   [2] Matt. 6. 5.
[3] Acts 16. 25.   [4] Acts 27. 35.   [5] Acts 2. 15.
[6] Acts 10. 9.   [7] Acts 3. 1.   [8] Dan. 6. 10.

advenam, ne angelus forte sit. sed nec ipse a fratribus excep*tus*
priora fece*ris* refrigeria terrena caelestibus: statim enim iudicabitur
5 fides tua. aut quomodo secundum praeceptum Pax huic domui
dices, nisi et eis qui in domo sunt pacem mutuam reddas?

27 Diligentiores in orando subiungere in orationibus alleluia
solent et hoc genus psalmos, quorum clausulis respondeant qui
simul sunt: et est optimum utique institutum omn*i* quod prae-
ponendo et honorando deo competit saturatam orationem velut
5 op*i*mam hostiam admovere.

28 Haec est enim hostia spiritalis quae pristina sacrificia delevit.
Quo mihi, inquit, multitudinem sacrificiorum vestrorum? plenus
sum holocaustomatum arietum, et adipem agnorum et sanguinem taurorum et hircorum nolo: quis enim requisivit ista de
5 manibus vestris? quae ergo quaesierit deus evangelium docet:
Veniet hora, inquit, cum veri adoratores adorabunt patrem in
spiritu et veritate: deus enim spiritus est et adoratores itaque tales
requirit. nos sumus veri adoratores et veri sacerdotes, qui spiritu
orantes spiritu sacrificamus orationem, hostiam dei propriam et
10 acceptabilem, quam scilicet requisivit, quam sibi prospexit. hanc
de toto corde devotam, fide pastam, veritate curatam, innocentia
integram, castitate mundam, agape coronatam, cum pompa
operum bonorum inter psalmos et hymnos deducere ad dei altare
debemus omnia nobis a deo impetraturam.

29 Quid enim orationi de spiritu et veritate venienti nega*bit* deus
qui eam exigit? legimus et audimus et credimus quanta docu-

26: 3 exceptus *x* exceptis *D*.
    4 feceris *scripsi* fecerit *D edd. praeter Diercks*.
27: 3 omni *scripsi (ita et Diercks)* omne *D*.
    5 opimam *x* optimam *D*.
28: 7 itaque *D edd.: quaero an scribendum* utique.
29: 1 negabit *x* negavit *D*.

especially a stranger, lest perchance he be an angel.[1] And yourself, when received as guest by the brethren, give not earthly
refreshment precedence over heavenly: for your faith will
inevitably come under judgement. Or how shall you, according
to the precept, say *Peace be to this house*,[2] unless you also bring
peace to those in the house and receive it as a gift from them?

27 The more conscientious in prayer are accustomed to append
to their prayers *Alleluia* and such manner of psalms, so that those
who are present may respond with the endings of them. And it is
certainly an excellent custom to present, like a rich oblation,[3]
a prayer fattened with all that conduces to setting forth the dignity
and honour of God.

28 For this is the spiritual oblation[4] which has wiped out the
ancient sacrifices. *To what purpose,* he says, *is the multitude of your
sacrifices unto me? I am full of whole burnt offerings of rams: and the
fat of lambs and the blood of bulls and he-goats I will not. For who hath
sought after these things at your hands?*[5] What things then God has
asked for, the Gospel teaches: *The hour will come,* he says, *when
the true worshippers shall worship the Father in the Spirit and the Truth.*
For *God is Spirit* and therefore *seeks after worshippers of this sort.*[6]
We are the true worshippers and the true priests, who, praying in
the Spirit,[7] in the Spirit offer a sacrifice of prayer[8] as an oblation
which is God's own and is well pleasing ⟨to him⟩, that in fact
which he has sought after,[9] which he has provided for himself.[10]
This, devoted from the whole heart, fatted by faith, prepared by
the truth, unmutilated in innocency, pure in chastity, garlanded
with charity, it is our duty to bring to the altar of God, along with
a procession of good works, to the accompaniment of psalms and
hymns,[11] as that which will obtain for us from God all that we
ask for.

29 For what will God deny to a prayer which proceeds from the
Spirit and the Truth, seeing it is he who demands this?[12] We read

---

[1] Cf. Heb. 13. 2.   [2] Luke 10. 5; cf. Matt. 10. 12.
[3] Cf. Ps. 141. 2.   [4] 1 Pet. 2. 5.   [5] Isa. 1. 11, 12.
[6] John 4. 23, 24.   [7] 1 Cor. 14. 15.   [8] Heb. 13. 15, 16.
[9] Deut. 10. 12; Mic. 6. 8.   [10] Gen. 22. 8, 13; cf. Heb. 10. 5.
[11] Eph. 5. 19; Col. 3. 16.   [12] John 4. 24.

menta efficaciae eius. vetus quidem oratio et ab ignibus et a bestiis
et ab inedia liberabat, et tamen non a Christo acceperat formam.
5 ceterum quanto amplius operatur oratio Christiana. non roris
angelum in mediis ignibus sistit nec ora leonibus obstruit nec
esurientibus rusticorum prandium transfert: nullum sensum
passionis delegata gratia avertit, sed patientes et sentientes et
dolentes sufferentia instruit: virtute ampliat gratiam, ut sciat fides
10 quid a domino consequatur, intellegens quid pro dei nomine
patiatur. sed et retro oratio plagas inrogabat, fundebat hostium
exercitus, imbrium utilia prohibebat: nunc vero oratio iustitiae
omnem iram dei avertit, pro inimicis excubat, pro persequentibus
supplicat. mirum si aquas caelestes extorquere novit, quae potuit
15 et ignes impetrare? sola est oratio quae deum vincit. sed Christus
eam nihil mali voluit operari: omnem illi virtutem de bono
contulit. itaque nihil novit nisi defunctorum animas de ipso mortis
itinere revocare, debiles reformare, aegros remediare, demoniacos
expiare, claustra carceris aperire, vincula innocentium solvere.
20 eadem diluit delicta, temptationes repellit, persecutiones extinguit,
pusillanimos consolatur, magnanimos oblectat, peregrinantes
deducit, fluctus mitigat, latrones obstupefacit, alit pauperes, regit
divites, lapsos erigit, cadentes suspendit, stantes continet. oratio
murus est fidei, arma et tela nostra adversus hostem qui nos
25 undique observat. itaque nunquam inermes incedamus: die
stationis, nocte vigiliae meminerimus. sub armis orationis signum
nostri imperatoris custodiamus: tubam angeli exspectemus oran-

---

29: 5 operatur *x* oratur *D*.
    16 voluit *x* novit *D*   Christianus ea nihil mali novit operari *placuit qui-*
    busdam quos Oeh. *non nomine laudat: attamen scribere* omnem illi virtutem
    ⟨deus⟩ *quoque debuissent.*
    18 revocare *x* vocare *D*.
    24 hostem *x* hominem *D*.

and hear and believe how great are the evidences of its efficacy. The old prayer, no doubt, brought deliverance from fire and wild beasts and hunger, while yet it had not received its pattern from Christ: then how much more fully operative is the Christian prayer! It does not establish the angel of the dew in the midst of the fire,[1] nor block the mouths of lions,[2] nor transfer to the hungry the peasants' dinner.[3] It turns away by delegated grace no perception of suffering, yet it arms with endurance those who do suffer and perceive and grieve. It makes grace multiply in power, so that faith may know what it obtains from the Lord, while it understands what for God's name's sake it is suffering. Moreover, of old time prayer induced plagues,[4] put to flight the hosts of the enemy,[5] withheld the benefits of rain:[6] now however the prayer of righteousness turns aside the whole wrath of God, keeps watch on behalf of foes, makes supplication for persecutors. Is it surprising that it knows how to squeeze out the waters of heaven, seeing it did have power even to ask for fire and obtain it?[7] Prayer alone it is that conquers God. But it was Christ's wish for it to work no evil:[8] he has conferred upon it all power concerning good. And so its only knowledge is how to call back the souls of the deceased from the very highway of death,[9] to straighten the feeble,[10] to heal the sick,[11] to cleanse the devil-possessed,[12] to open the bars of the prison,[13] to loose the bands of the innocent.[14] It also absolves sins, drives back temptations, quenches persecutions, strengthens the weak-hearted, delights the high-minded, brings home wayfarers, soothes the waves, astounds robbers, feeds the poor, rules the rich, lifts up the fallen, supports the unstable, upholds them that stand. Prayer is the bulwark of faith, our defensive and offensive armour against the enemy who is watching us from every side. So let us never proceed unarmed: by day let us remember the station, by night the vigil. Beneath the armour of prayer let us guard our Emperor's standard: let us

---

[1] Dan. 3. 49, 50. LXX. Thdt.   [2] Dan. 6. 22; cf. Heb. 11. 33.
[3] Bel and Dragon 33.   [4] 2 Kings 6. 18.   [5] Heb. 11. 34.
[6] Jas. 5. 17.   [7] 2 Kings 1. 10 etc.   [8] Luke 9. 54–56.
[9] Acts 9. 36–41.   [10] Acts 3. 7.   [11] Acts 9. 32.
[12] Acts 16. 18.   [13] Acts 12. 10.   [14] Acts 16. 26.

tes. orant etiam angeli omnes, orat omnis creatura. orant pecudes
et ferae et genua declinant, et egredientes de stabulis et speluncis
30 ad caelum non otiosi ore suspiciunt vibrantes spiritum suo more.
sed et aves nunc exsurgentes eriguntur ad caelum, et alarum crucem
pro manibus expandunt et dicunt aliquid quod oratio videatur.
quid ergo amplius de officio orationis? etiam ipse dominus oravit:
cui sit honor et virtus in saecula saeculorum.

29: 30 otiosi *D* otioso *Mur.*   suo more *x* suo movere *D.*
   31 nunc *D* nido *x* mane *Reiff.*

pray while waiting for the angel's trumpet. Even the angels pray, all of them. The whole creation prays. Cattle and wild beasts pray, and bend their knees, and in coming forth from their stalls and lairs look up to heaven, their mouth not idle, making the spirit move in their own fashion. Moreover the birds now arising are lifting themselves up to heaven and instead of hands are spreading out the cross of their wings, while saying something which may be supposed to be a prayer. What more then of the obligation of prayer? Even the Lord himself prayed: to him be honour and power for ever and ever.

NOTES

1 **Dei spiritus etc.** From the text 'God is a spirit' (John 4. 24) Tertullian deduces that 'spirit' is a term descriptive of the divine Substance, applicable to all or each of the divine Persons. Thus, with many other ancient interpreters, he equates 'The Spirit of God shall come upon thee' (Luke 1. 35, as he read the text) with 'The Word was made flesh' (John 1. 14), and contends that 'Spirit' in this case means the divine Word, the second Person of the holy Trinity. This does not mean that Tertullian in any sense identifies the second and third Persons of the holy Trinity, but only that the texts quoted are interpreted by him as identical in meaning. In this of course he was mistaken. What the text from Luke means, as other fathers point out, is that it was by the operation of the Holy Spirit that the virginal conception took place. By this miracle the Temple of the Lord's body was brought into being. How the Lord entered into his Temple is a mystery too great even for evangelists to look into. Sound theology, however, requires us to acknowledge that at no point of its natal or pre-natal existence was that Temple without its divine Inhabitant. For Tertullian's argument cf. *Adv. Praxean* 26.

1 **sermo et ratio.** 'Word' and 'reason' are alternative renderings of the Greek λόγος (John 1. 1–14), which has both these meanings and several others. Tertullian elsewhere observes (*Adv. Prax.* 5) that 'speech' and 'reason' are not so much alternative as complementary renderings, in that reason is prior to speech, yet is inconceivable except as a kind of unspoken speech. The second clause of the present sentence is therefore more than playing with words: it indicates that this mutual relation between Speech and Reason is inherent in the Being of God, and thus (as he will

proceed to say) manifests itself in every part of God's revelation, including the Lord's Prayer.

2 spiritus utrumque is the reading of the manuscripts, and as it makes sense there seems no need to alter it. If any alteration were called for, I should prefer to read *utrimque*, and translate 'in either case spirit'. Some editors, reading *utriusque*, suggest the sense 'the spirit of both'. This can hardly be right, for in Tertullian's view Spirit is not in either possessive or partitive dependence on the divine Word or Reason, but is his 'substance', that which he essentially is.

3 novis. So Pamelius corrected the MS. *nobis*—'to us the disciples'. In the Middle Ages there was a tendency for B to be pronounced as V (as in modern Spanish) or as W (as in modern Syriac), and thus, as the critical notes will show, the copyists frequently confuse such forms as *amavit* and *amabit*.

3 orationis formam, 'plan of prayer'. *Forma* means (*a*) a rule of law, a precedent or standing order, (*b*) an architect's blueprint or a surveyor's plan. The latter meaning seems more in keeping with the verb *determinavit*, 'has marked out'. But the former is within reach of the author's mind, as the next sentence shows.

4 in hac quoque specie, 'in this case also'. *Species* as a legal term means the particular application of the requisite *forma* or general rule.

9 superducto evangelio, 'by the subsequent addition of the Gospel'. This is the meaning favoured by Diercks, who discusses a number of views. There may, however, be a reminiscence of 2 Corinthians 5. 2–4, where it is said that the carnal will be transmuted to spiritual by being clothed upon by that which is from heaven: so perhaps translate, 'by being clothed upon with the Gospel'. In 2 Cor., however, the verb is *superindui*. *Superinducticios fratres* is quoted by Tertullian (*Adv. Marc.* v. 3) from Galatians 2. 4, where it is used in an unfavourable sense, of sneaking interlopers.

9 expunctore, 'fulfiller'. *Expungere* commonly, though not invariably, means 'complete' or 'bring to perfection'. See a further note on § 9.

12 ratio quo venit is the MS. reading. The editors have changed *quo* to *qua*, and have expressed doubt as to the correctness of *venit*, which indeed does not seem to have any very apposite meaning. I have restored *quo*, which in all three clauses, and again below, stands for *quod* or *quoniam*. *Qua* is manifestly wrong: Tertullian does not say that in the Gospel our Lord is set forth as the spirit by which he was strong, etc., but that he is shown to be spirit (i.e. the divine substance) in that he was strong, and so forth. For *venit* I have ventured to write *intervenit*, supposing a reference to a further sense of *ratio*, which (like λόγος) can signify a geometrical mean, and thus suggest the idea of mediation. Tertullian several times quotes the text 'one mediator of God and men' (1 Timothy 2. 5), and it may have been in his mind here. At *Apol.* 17 we have, in reference to God the Father, *ratione qua disposuit*, and again, ibid. 21, *ratio adsit disponenti*, which may have some bearing on the present passage.

14 ex ratione quo reconciliat. This clause is not in the MS., though evidently some reference to *ratio* is required to complete the sentence. Pamelius supplied *ex ratione qua docetur*, which seems unlikely in view of *docuerat* following. Rigaltius preferred *suscipitur*, 'by which it is apprehended', which involves a subjectivism alien to Tertullian's thought. In such a case one man's guess is likely to be as good as another's, and I have preferred to write *reconciliat*, with a back-reference to my previous suggestion *intervenit*—the Word mediates, the prayer ordained by him reconciles.

17 cum ipso spiritu. There seems to be a reference to 2 Kings 2. 15, 'The spirit of Elijah doth rest upon Elisha', as well as to Luke 1. 15 and 3. 22. Justin Martyr (*Dial.* 87), interpreting Isaiah 11. 2, 'the Spirit of the Lord shall rest upon him', makes 'rest' mean 'cease', and points out that after the coming of Christ Jewish prophecy did cease. In the same work (§ 51) he has already said that when Christ came he caused John to cease from prophesying and baptizing. Tertullian expresses this idea in stronger terms, *Adv. Marc.* iv. 18: *ipso iam domino virtutum sermone et spiritu patris operante in terris et praedicante, necesse erat* *portionem spiritus sancti, quae ex forma prophetici moduli in Ioanne egerat praeparaturam viarum dominicarum, abscedere iam a Ioanne, redactam scilicet in dominum ut in massalem suam summam.* So also *Adv. Iud.* 8: *omnis plenitudo spiritalium retro charismatum in Christo cesserunt* (where read *cessarunt*).

18 in quae verba: a legal phrase for a dictated form of oath or verbal undertaking.

26 modestiam fidei, here and a little later, seems to mean the effect of faith in restricting worship to its only proper object, and keeping its expression within reasonable bounds. So again in § 17, of restraint in gesture and attitude.

27 sequente sophia, the MS. reading, has been tampered with by some of the editors. Quintilian (with whose work Tertullian was acquainted) several times uses *primum...sequens...tertium* for the terms of an enumeration: e.g. *Inst. Orat.* vii. 9. 9, *verum id quod ex his primum est mutatione casuum, sequens divisione verborum aut translatione emendatur, tertium adiectione.* So here, *sequente sophia* connects with *imprimis* and *ad tertium sophiae gradum*: and the subject of *pertineat* is the clause *si non agmine verborum etc.*

32 substantia, a late Latin word, first quoted from Quintilian, is evidently a translation of the Greek ὑπόστασις, and capable of taking on almost any of the many meanings of that word. The sense here is perhaps of firm ground underfoot, as in LXX of Psalm 69. 2, 'I stick fast in the deep mire where no ground is', or (metaphorically) at Hebrews 11. 1, 'certainty concerning things hoped for'. Or possibly the meaning is 'is sustained by the wealth of a great and opulent interpretation'. See a further note on § 4.

CHAPTER II

1 testimonio dei, 'our witness to God', an objective genitive.

1 merito fidei, literally 'desert of faith', but by metonymy the work by which the merit is acquired.

13 mater ecclesia. This is apparently the earliest appearance of this expression, which however has an obvious origin in Galatians

4. 26, and was evidently not unknown to Tertullian's audience. The language here is too abbreviated to be quite clear, and the thought is somewhat confused: but probably Tertullian does not mean that the relation between God the Father and God the Son implies the Church as mother, but that Christians, in calling upon God as their father, acknowledge the Church as their mother. The suggestion of some commentators that the Church here means the Holy Spirit is quite alien to Tertullian's thought. Cf. *De Pudicitia* 21, where the three divine Persons are described as an *ecclesia*; and *De Bapt.* 6, *cum autem sub tribus et testatio fidei* (the creed) *et sponsio salutis* (the baptismal formula) *pigneretur, necessario adicitur ecclesiae mentio, quoniam ubi tres, id est pater et filius et spiritus sanctus, ibi ecclesia quae trium corpus est.* On *mater ecclesia* see a monograph by J. C. Plumpe, Washington, D.C., 1943.

14 **uno genere aut vocabulo.** Literally 'one genus or word'.

CHAPTER III

2 **aliud quidem nomen audierat.** Tertullian means that 'Father' is, so to speak, the personal name of God, a kind of proper name such as was asked after by Jacob (Gen. 32. 29), Moses (Ex. 3. 13), and Manoah (Judges 13. 17). Two of these received no answer. Moses did receive an answer, but it was not this name 'Father' but another name 'I am that I am'. Compare above § 2, 'when we say *Father* we also give God a [or his] name'.

3 **iam enim filius etc.** The MS. text is in some confusion. This restoration by Gelenius has at least the advantage of making sense and of being in harmony with what follows and with what Tertullian says elsewhere. Cf. *Adv. Prax.* 23, *Pater glorifica nomen tuum, in quo* (sc. *nomine*) *erat filius.* Strange as it may seem, Tertullian does mean that the Son in person (not the title 'son') is the Father's new name: which is true in that it is only through the Son that the Father may be known: cf. Matthew 11. 2; Luke 10. 22. 'New name', if it is correct, will be a reminiscence of Rev. 3. 12. I am disposed, however, to suggest that the true reading may

be, *iniquis enim filius non patris nomen est,* a parenthetic reference to the general tenor of John 5. 43–47 and 12. 37–43.

12 illa angelorum circumstantia. Rev. 7. 11 conflated with 4. 8 and Isaiah 6. 3.

14 angelorum candidati. Here and in other places Tertullian almost, but never entirely, lends himself to the erroneous idea that at the resurrection redeemed men will be transmuted into angels. At *De Res. Carn.* 36, commenting on Matthew 22. 30, he says, *similes enim erunt angelis qua non nupturi quia nec morituri, sed qua transituri in statum angelicum per indumentum illud incorruptibilitatis, per substantiae resuscitatae tamen demutationem.* He frequently recurs to the same theme. In the passage before us he need mean no more than that we shall be associated with the angels, joining with them in the divine praises: though he may also have in mind that other theory, the truth of which by the time of St Augustine was taken for axiomatic, that the purpose of God in creating mankind was to provide those who should fill up the places in heaven left vacant by the expulsion of Lucifer and his adherents. See Augustine, *Enchiridion* 62, *instaurantur quippe quae in caelis sunt cum id quod inde in angelis lapsum est in hominibus redditur.* This theme provides a large section of the argument of St Anselm, *Cur Deus Homo?*

CHAPTER IV

5 nos sumus caelum et terra. Cf. Augustine, *Enchiridion* 115, *sicut in caelo et in terra, quod non absurde quidam intellexerunt, in spiritu et in corpore.*

9 substantiam et facultatem, 'substance and possession'. In later legal Latin *substantia* means property, for which *facultas* is the classical term.

21 substantia passionis, 'by the suffering of the passion'. 'Suffer' is a well authenticated sense of the Greek verb ὑφίστασθαι, and is a conceivable meaning of the derived substantive ὑπόστασις and its Latin equivalent. The editors, not observing this, or not admitting it, are disposed to follow Ursinus in writing *sub* *instantiam passionis,* which is supposed to mean 'at the imminence of the passion'— though it is somewhat doubtful whether it does. Oehler retains *substantia,* but is wrong in his suggestion that it means nature, quality, and mode. If *substantia* is used in a metaphysical sense, 'nature' or 'quality' is not its meaning, for neither passion nor action nor any other function or attribute can be described as 'substance'.

CHAPTER V

6 protractum quendam saeculo. This, the reading of *A,* appears to give the required sense. *Pertractum* (*B*) occurs nowhere else, and could only mean forcible arrest. *Protractus* means extension or prolongation: *quendam* marks it as the actual word they used. Their prayer, however, was not that they should be allowed an extension of their time in this world (*in saeculo, B*), but that a longer existence should by granted to the world itself (*saeculo, A*). According to Tertullian (*Apol.* 39) Christians prayed *pro mora finis,* 'for the end to be delayed', so as to give unbelievers a longer space for repentance. The better authenticated prayer was 'Thy kingdom come', i.e. Let this world pass away, and the kingdom of God be established by Christ's appearing. See the last sentence of this chapter.

11 clamant ad dominum invidia, 'cry to the Lord in reproach'. The reference is to Rev. 6. 10, where there is a kind of suppressed undertone of reproach in the appeal 'How long?' Hartel's *ad domini iudicia* is therefore unnecessary: it is in keeping with 'Wilt thou not judge and avenge?', but would require not *clamant* but *provocant.* Too many of the editors' readings sap the vigour of Tertullian's language.

CHAPTER VI

4 edixerat, 'had stated the principle': Gelenius' correction of the MS. *ei dixerat.* The word suggests the praetor's edict by which, at the beginning of his year of office, he announced the principles on which justice would be administered in his court.

9 corpus eius in pane censetur. This sentence has been both the subject and the weapon of much controversy. It has been supposed to have a bearing on the question of the Real Presence of Christ in the Eucharist, and the verb *censetur* (taken as meaning 'is thought') has been seized upon by those who claim that there is merely a putative presence. But *censeri* in Tertullian never means 'to be thought to be', but always has in view the Roman census, the purpose of which was (*a*) to count numbers, (*b*) to estimate a citizen's rank in view of his birth, wealth, or the offices he has held, and (*c*) to assign to him a new rank from now on: and all this not as a matter of opinion or appearance or repute, but of objective authoritative fact. The second case is in point here, the dominical words 'This is my body' being equivalent to the censorial *aestimatio* and constituting an authoritative declaration that the Lord's body is in the rank or class of bread, i.e. is a species of food. A parallel phrase would be *in quattuordecim censetur*, a person is listed in the rank of *eques*. Moreover the present sentence has not, as far as Tertullian's immediate intention goes, any direct bearing on the theology of the Eucharist. He does not say that the Lord's body is either reputed to be, or officially declared to be, in the bread of the Eucharist—indeed either of these statements would seem to have more affinity with Lutheran than with catholic theology. What he does say is that the Lord's natural body is in some sense a kind of food, in view of such a text as 'My flesh is meat indeed' and others in John 6, and that the words of the Institution of the Eucharist are the authoritative official declaration of this. The reading *vitae panis* (Semler, Reifferscheid) is uncalled for, and spoils the argument, which is a syllogism in the third figure (*darapti*).

23 ea ipsa nocte moriturus. This concluding sentence is evidently faulty in the MS. The pronoun *is* is redundant and the clause has no link with what precedes. My reading seems to solve both these difficulties and to make an ending quite in Tertullian's style.

CHAPTER VII

1 Consequens erat etc., literally, 'it logically followed'. *Precari* more naturally takes an accusative of the person addressed than of the thing desired: so possibly we may suppose that the divine clemency is to some degree personified as the hearer of the prayer: almost 'address ourselves to his clemency'.

5 exomologesis. This Greek word was apparently in such common use among African Christians as to be intelligible even to the hearers of a sermon.

6 delictum confitetur, literally 'confesses the tort'. On this its second appearance in this passage, the term seems to be used in its legal sense, with a general application to all cases where a defendant asks pardon of the plaintiff or seeks the indulgence of the court. In the succeeding sentences its sense is restricted to offences against God, and it means 'sin', as commonly in ecclesiastical writers. A tort, *delictum*, is a wrong done not to the state or to society, but to a person: which makes it an appropriate word for offences against God, who is personal in himself and condescends to enter into personal relations with men. *Peccatum*, often a self-excusing word, looks at the sin from the standpoint of the one who fell into the error.

16 hac specie orationis, 'this clause of the prayer'. But possibly the sense is more general, 'this type of petition'.

CHAPTER VIII

1 tam expeditae orationis, a metaphor based on the convenience and quick movement of light-armed troops.

4 ne nos patiaris etc. According to Cyprian (*De Orat. Dom.* 25), the Ambrosian *De Sacram.* v. 4, and Augustine (*De Serm. in Monte* ii. 19), some churches actually did recite the clause in this form. Much of its difficulty disappears when we observe that usually in the New Testament, and perhaps here in the prayer, 'temptation' means not what we commonly understand by the term, but persecution, which is still (among men and boys who work with their fellows) a real temptation to apostasy.

6 infirmitas: 'weakness', i.e. ignorance, which is a form of weakness. Tertullian's audience are not the only people who have been disturbed by Gen. 22. 1, 'God did tempt (i.e. test) Abraham.'

7 iusserat. The point of the pluperfect is that, according to common patristic doctrine, the God of the theophanies is God the Son. He who had commanded Abraham to sacrifice his son was the same divine Person who afterwards said, 'He that loveth son or daughter more than me is not worthy of me.'

13 respondet clausula. It would be too much to suppose that the custom had already grown up of using the last two clauses of the prayer as a versicle and response. Cyprian, and Cyril of Jerusalem, mention no such custom. The Ambrosian *De Sacramentis* passes over the last clause, which may conceivably at Milan have become detached from the prayer by being made into a response.

CHAPTER IX

3 expunguntur, 'are summed up', a term of accountancy. The verb occurs again in § 11 meaning 'give effect to', and in § 1 we have *expunctor*, 'fulfiller'.

8 religio orationis, 'the sanctity of the prayer'. *Religio* has something of the meaning involved in the modern word 'numinosity', though with much more of conscious intelligence than this term usually implies. In § 6 it occurs in the complementary subjective sense of 'reverence'.

CHAPTER X

5 accedentium desideriorum. Whatever the position of *ius est* (see the critical note) it is more natural to take these genitives as dependent on *petitiones*, 'petitions concerned with additional desires'. It is, however, just possible, reading with *D*, to take them with *fundamento*, 'as a foundation of additional desires'.

6 ne quantum etc. Diercks rightly, as it appears, joins this
clause with what precedes. Other editors make it the beginning
of § 11.

CHAPTER XI

8 ne irascamini: Gen. 45. 24. This, Driver observes, is the
correct meaning of the Hebrew expression which the English
versions represent by 'fall not out', a phrase which apparently
had the same colloquial meaning in the sixteenth century as it
had in the late nineteenth, 'quarrel'.

9 disciplina nostratum: Diercks' brilliant correction of the
MSS. and editors' *nostra tum*. At *Scorpiace* 10, *nostrates homines*, in
the mouth of Valentinians, means 'men as we know them', as
distinguished from certain supposed ideal or transcendental men:
Adv. Marc. v. 16, *nostratem deum* is a God such as Christians believe
in, as opposed to the merely amiable god of Marcion. Neither of
these is strictly parallel with the present: but unless Diercks'
suggestion is accepted, *tum* is redundant and makes no sense.
Disciplina, 'doctrine', perhaps means 'school', as we say 'school of
thought' or 'school of philosophy'. The reference is to Acts 9. 2
and similar texts.

11 superponit, 'equates'. What Tertullian means, as Muratorius
observes, is that whereas anger was not condemned in the Law but
homicide was, our Lord adds (which is the actual meaning of
superponit) his own condemnation of anger to the Mosaic condemnation of homicide.

CHAPTER XII

2 tali spiritu. 'Holy Spirit' throughout this passage, as often
in Tertullian, means God, without distinction of Persons: see
a note on § 1. The insertion of the preposition before *spiritu sancto*
seems justified by its occurrence later in the sentence. In any case
we should have wondered at its omission, for 'spirit' to Tertullian
is never less than personal.

CHAPTER XIII

1 quae ratio est, 'what sense is there?' Cf. *Adv. Prax.* 18 where *habet rationem* means 'the scripture is right', as in the modern French idiom.

1 spiritus in this passage is used almost in the modern sense of the English word 'soul'. In Greek and in Latin 'soul' (ψυχή, *anima*) has no necessary moral or religious connotation, being the life-principle in plants and animals as well as men. Tertullian and the church writers attach the moral and religious connotation to 'spirit', as does St Paul. But it is through 'soul' that 'spirit' influences the whole personality, and thus in a secondary sense 'soul' obtains a moral content.

3 a falso etc. These are not a series of vaguely apprehended misdoings or misthinkings, but each of the words refers to some definite crime which is condemned by the legal code or by the laws of Christian morality, and in which the hands play some part. *Veneficia*, sorcery, is the making of charms and philtres: *idololatria* would include the fabrication, as well as the worship, of idols.

7 aquam sumere appears to be a standing phrase for partial washings or rinsings: it occurs several times in Ovid. 'A bath of the whole body' seems not to refer (as some commentators think) to Baptism, though there is such a reference at the end of this chapter. Contrary to common opinion, the early Christians, like their heathen neighbours, did quite frequently wash themselves: it was among the ascetics of the fourth century, and in the Middle Ages, that dirt became a sign of godliness.

9 Pilati: manus abluisse. The express reference to Pilate is omitted in two of the three primary authorities, which read 'to be a recollection to the Lord's deliverance'. The sentence however reads lamely without the additional words, and they should almost certainly be retained, but punctuated as in my text. The omission of the subject of the infinitive is not unparalleled, and is in this case a stylistic improvement.

11 nisi ob aliquod etc. The text here is doubtful. An alternative pair of readings would give 'unless some defilement of human conversation become a matter of conscience'. This would involve taking *nisi quod* from *AB* and omitting *lavemus* with *AD*. The meaning seems to be that ceremonial washings for the sake of ceremony are to be deprecated, but that a rinsing of the hands is permissible if it expresses a desire to cleanse the conscience of some fault lately contracted. *Conversatio* is 'conversation' in the English New Testament sense of that word, for which there is no satisfactory modern equivalent: it means both the circumstances in which a person lives, his attitude in regard to them, and his conduct in view of them: 'behaviour' by no means meets the case.

CHAPTER XIV

3 conscientia patrum, 'through consciousness of their fathers' guilt'. The expression combines the ideas of consciousness, self-consciousness, cognizance, and conscience. They feel themselves to be sinners because they acknowledge that their fathers were.

6 dominica passione modulantes. The text is difficult, and the editors have made many suggestions for its improvement, none of them very plausible. I read as in the text, taking *manus* as the object of the participle. *Modulari* means to express by mimicry, as in ancient dancing: cf. Pliny, *H.N.* ii. 95 [*insulae*] *saltuares dictae quoniam in symphoniae cantu ad ictus modulantium pedum moventur*. The supine (as in *AD*) without a verb of motion is not impossible, though unusual, but would require *dominicam passionem*: conceivably this is the correct reading. The sense is the same in either case.

CHAPTER XV

9 de habitu orandi, 'of demeanour during prayer'. *Habitus*, ἕξις, means one's general attitude of mind, of body, of posture, though both here and in § 20 dress is intended, and little more.

CHAPTER XVI

1 assignata oratione, 'at the sealing of the prayer'. From what follows it appears that this does not mean the bidding or announcement of the prayer, but 'when the prayer is ended'. *Assignare* then must refer to some act which marked the conclusion of the prayer, e.g. the *pax* or the sign of the cross: cf. § 18, 'the kiss of peace, which is the seal of the prayer'.

3 Hermas and his book were held in high regard by popular Christian opinion, and in some quarters *The Shepherd* was almost reckoned as canonical scripture—a view against which the compiler of the ·Muratorian Canon thought it necessary to protest. Tertullian by no means agreed with the common judgement, and his belittling expressions here reflect his general attitude. Cf. *De Pud.* 20, *illo apocrypho Pastore moechorum*, which only means that Hermas professed to have received divine pardon for one mildly lascivious thought, on condition that it was never repeated.

5 ad observationem is equivalent to *ad observandum*: Tertullian not infrequently uses the verbal substantive for the gerund. More commonly, as *observare* is to keep a rule, *observatio* is a rule that ought to be kept.

9 cathedra, the chair, is the bishop's throne: *subsellium*, the bench, is the seats for the presbyters.

16 angelo orationis adstante. There may be a reference to Tobit 12. 12, though more probably to Luke 1. 11 or Rev. 8. 3, 4. Tertullian ascribes much to the holy angels: e.g. *De Bapt.* 6, he says that the heavenly minister present at Baptism is an angel who by the remission of sins prepares the way for the Holy Spirit in confirmation, as the Baptist did by the baptism of water prepare the way for Christ to baptize with the Spirit and with fire. In truth, of course, our Lord is the Minister of every sacrament.

CHAPTER XVII

13 qui clarius adorant. The Latin indicates, as the translation is intended to indicate, that there were people then present in the congregation who were at that moment praying, or had recently been praying, in a loud voice. The habit of listening to the sermon quietly had not at that date been evolved: generally speaking it is a post-reformation practice.

CHAPTER XVIII

1 ieiunantes etc. The fasts here referred to are evidently of private devotion, not those prescribed by custom or imposed by authority. The regular fasting days were Wednesdays and Fridays (known as station days), on which also there was a church service, either the Eucharist entire or the earlier part of it, consisting of psalms, scripture reading, instruction, and prayers. The kiss of peace (often referred to briefly as *pax*, 'the peace') was exchanged at the end of the prayers. At Rome in the second century (as Justin Martyr relates, and Hippolytus in the third century agrees) the *pax* followed those earlier prayers which preceded the offertory. A relic of those prayers still stands in the Latin Mass in the *Oremus* which follows the Gospel or the Creed, though apparently no prayers are said at that point except on Good Friday. At Rome since the fourth century the *pax* has come after the Canon. When the change took place is not clear, but it may even have been made by the reforming popes Zephyrinus and Callistus, against whose policy Hippolytus' Church Order is in some sort a protest.

3 nisi cum oratio etc. The text here is doubtful, and the MS. testimony in some confusion. Diercks' brilliant *cum oratio operatione* makes sense of the beginning of the sentence. I take *maduerint* from *D*, but have written *qui* where *D* has *qua*. *Madere* for 'break the fast' is obvious, since fasting in Greek is ξηροφαγία, 'dry eating'. The end of the sentence is more difficult, *transigendus*, *-o*, *-um* being meaningless. I am not very pleased with my suggestion, but have ventured to write *transferendo*, with the meaning indicated in the translation. *De sua pace* is equivalent to a sort of partitive genitive, though with a retained sense of ablative of origin. The last five words of the sentence must be construed with *participent*, not with *qui maduerint*. The meaning seems to be that the brethren who are not fasting will, by communicating their peace to the brother who is, receive in exchange some of the merit of his 'good work'.

15 die paschae. Good Friday was observed as a forty hours' fast, beginning at sunset on Thursday and ending on Saturday. In the Roman rite the *pax* is still omitted on Good Friday.

CHAPTER XIX

1 sacrificiorum orationes are the consecration prayer of the Eucharist, i.e. all that follows the Offertory. The primitive Church knew nothing of what is now known as non-communicating attendance, and the proposal to which Tertullian here takes exception was that, as these people did not intend to communicate, they should retire from the service before the Offertory. *Ara* is a most unusual word for a Christian (or the Jewish) altar, the usual word being *altare*. If classical analogy is any guide, in Christian usage *altare* would mean the Lord's Table (as in fact it often does) while *ara* would mean the place on which it stands, and the space surrounding it. On the practice of private reservation see the Introduction, p. xv.

CHAPTER XX

1 De habitu etc. The reference is to one or both of the two books *De Cultu Feminarum*, of which the former, beginning with a reminiscence of the opening line of Juvenal's sixth satire, surpasses in offensiveness even that notorious work. The second is somewhat less objectionable. In the present passage Tertullian in the one word *operositatem* sums up a whole sentence of St Peter. The variant reading *morositatem*, 'nicety', 'punctiliousness', would mean much the same thing, but with reference to the state of the lady's mind rather than the skill of her maid's hands. At *De Cult. Fem.* ii. 7 we have *ordinandi crinis operositas*.

CHAPTER XXI

1 Sed, quod promisce etc. There is a double anacoluthon in this sentence, as indicated in the translation: *quasi incertum* cannot be attached to *observatur*, for an *observatio* is a rule which ought to be, and in general is being, kept, and there is nothing uncertain about it. Those who wished to disregard the rule were a very small group, and Tertullian seems, if not to have persuaded them, at least to have made them conform.

CHAPTER XXII

5 feminam...specialiter. This clause, 'female in respect of the sex generically, woman in respect of the rank of the sex specifically', seems to contradict the whole tenor of Tertullian's argument, and should almost certainly be omitted, though the editors (except Diercks) retain it.

22 et virgo contingitur. Some editors suggest *continetur*, 'is included', but wrongly, for in Latin 'sex' is not (as it used to be in English) a collective noun, but a noun of quality.

27 nec viri non velandi: 'so too of the man, who must not have his head covered'. This is the best I can make of this group of words, which in the MS. are quite unintelligible.

50 defendit, 'makes immune', could conceivably mean 'protects from masculine attentions and the risks consequent upon them'. This, however, does not seem to have occurred to the editors, and it may perhaps be more safe to interpret, 'protects from the Pauline law regarding dress', though in that case one would have expected *excusat*. Elsewhere *defendere* means to repel, to defend, to avenge, or to maintain in argument: for which last see the following sentence.

53 excusetur nunc aetas. I had anticipated Diercks in making a period after *velamentum*. *Excusetur* is concessive, 'though it should be excused'. *Privilegium*, a privilege, is a private law, applying to a few named individuals or a specific group or class.

Tertullian insists that the fact that Eve and Adam covered themselves on the loss of their innocency is a precedent for his ruling
that when innocency passes away at puberty, so does its private
exemption from the general law.

58 resignantur, 'are carried forward', a term of accountancy:
an ante-classical use, vouched for by the grammarians. The
classical term is *rescribere*.

61 totum virginis praestet, 'show herself in every respect
a virgin'. So the MS. and the editors. But this is not in keeping
with Tertullian's argument, and I suggest we should read *totum
mulieris*, 'in every respect a woman'. He surely means that a dedi-
cated virgin admits her adult status by putting her hair up and
lengthening her skirts and wearing the *strophium*: so let her complete the process by wearing the head-covering. In so doing she
will keep her profession a secret between herself and God.

63 quod dei gratia exerceat. Some editors apparently object to
the idea that God's grace is itself an operative agent, and read
exerceamus or *exerceatur*, so that the meaning may be 'the works
performed for God's sake'. But above § 3 and *De Bapt.* 20 we
have *quos gratia dei exspectat*: if God's grace attends, why should it
not operate? An author must be allowed to develop his own
theological concepts.

78 ne compellantur etc. The translation given is the best I can
make of this very confused sentence, which editorial attempts at
emendation have not succeeded in improving.

83 expaverint. 'Bashfully experience' is a substantial softening
of the meaning of the Latin. The ancient practice of marrying
girls of thirteen to men whom they hardly knew and for whom
they could have no possible affection continued in Christian
Europe during many centuries. The fact that even a Christian
teacher could use this word without condemning the practice
which justified it, is the strongest ancient testimony I know to
the natural hardness of the human heart.

CHAPTER XXIII

2 quae dissensio etc. *Cum maxime* commonly means 'at this present moment': but here *cum* must be a conjunction, or the following clause will be out of connexion. There was of course at that date no formal trial of, or judgement on, these trivial but apparently important matters of dissension. They settled themselves in due course, by the common sense of the churches.

8 spatium pentecostes is the fifty days between Easter and Whitsunday, during which every day is a holy day. The 'day of the Lord's resurrection' means every Sunday, not Easter only.

CHAPTER XXIV

6 aut a Paulo seems a necessary correction of the MS. reading *apud Paulum*, though there is still some awkwardness, seeing that St Paul was one of the two already referred to as praying in the hearing of the guards. At Acts 27. 35 the Greek has εὐχαρίστησεν. Whether the food taken on the ship was intended by the apostle, or understood by the writer of the Acts, to be a Eucharist, may be a matter of doubt: Tertullian evidently thought, or wished to give the impression that he thought, that it was.

CHAPTER XXV

1 extrinsecus observatio, 'observance from external sources'. The verbal nouns are to Tertullian quite as much verbs as substantives and naturally enough take a qualifying adverb. See a note on § 16.

3 sollemniores, 'in established use'. This is what Diercks says the word means, and (after some hesitation) I agree. But cf. § 23, *eadem sollemnitate dispungitur*, which suggests that the meaning here may be 'of rather greater solemnity'.

5 communitatis omnis, 'everything common'. Tertullian's summary phrase for the unclean meats mentioned at Acts 10. 12, with a forward reference to 'common or unclean' in vv. 14

and 28. But as St Peter's vision was a parable of the ingathering of the gentiles, 'the whole Christian community' is also meant. Tertullian's intention was to suggest both.

CHAPTER XXVI

2 Vidisti fratrem etc. seems to be quoted as though it were scripture. Its source has not been identified.

CHAPTER XXVII

3 omne of the MS. must either be corrected to *omni* or read as equivalent to it.

CHAPTER XXVIII

10 hanc de toto corde etc. The participles in this sentence indicate successive stages in the ritual preparation of the victim for sacrifice: the qualifying ablatives specify the manner in which, in spiritual terms, these ritual requirements are met.

CHAPTER XXIX

14 aquas caelestes extorquere, 'squeeze out', as from a sponge. This may refer to the story, alluded to *Apol.* 5, that an army perishing of thirst on the German frontier (an unlikely enough contingency) was saved by rain which fell in answer to the prayers of some Christian soldiers. In that case, by contrast, the fire will be that which Elijah called down to consume the captains and their fifties. Or conceivably the rain is that which fell after the sacrifice at Carmel: in which case the fire will be that which had consumed the sacrifice.

31 aves nunc exsurgentes, 'the birds at this moment arising'. *Nunc* cannot mean *iam*: it refers strictly to the time when it is used. Tertullian's homily, if delivered during the eucharistic service, will have begun before daybreak. As he reaches this point the chatter of the early birds is heard along with the preacher's voice. The alterations *nido* and *mane*, the latter certainly rather flat, are therefore unnecessary.

INDEX OF SCRIPTURAL AND OTHER
REFERENCES

References are to chapter and line.

INDEX VERBORUM LATINORUM

reservare **19**. 5
residere **16**. 11
resignare **22**. 58
resolvere **19**. 4
retentio delictorum **11**. 5
retractare **6**. 15
retro (=antea) **1**. 6, 9; **29**. 11
revelare **3**. 3

sacrificare **8**. 7
sacrificium (=eucharistia) **18**. 7; **19**. 1
sanctificare **3**. 11, 12
sapientia divina **6**. 1
scandalum **23**. 4
scrupulose **13**. 8
secrete **1**. 23
securitas **6**. 22; **22**. 80
secus **4**. 19
sensus **1**. 33; **4**. 6
sequens (=secundus) **1**. 27, 28
sermo **1**. 1, 10, 11, 13, 35
sexus **21, 22** *passim*
si forte **18**. 11
sigillaria **16**. 10
signaculum **18**. 2
simplicitas **22**. 54
simpliciter **4**. 6; **16**. 5; **25**. 8
sollemnis **19**. 4; **25**. 3
sophia **1**. 23, 27, 31
specialiter **21**. 9
species **1**. 4; **7**. 16; **22**. 37, 44
spiritalis **1**. 8; **6**. 13; **13**. 2
spiritaliter **6**. 6
spiritus (dei) **1**. 1, 10, 11, 13, 18; **9**. 9;
  12. 3; **20**. 6; **22**. 8; **25**. 4; **28**. 8, 9;
  29. 1
spiritus (hominum) **4**. 5; **12**. 2, 4; **13**.
  1, 4; **22**. 85; **25**. 18
spiritus (pecudum) **29**. 30
statio **19**. 1, 2, 4, 7, 8; **23**. 11
status **22**. 1

sternere **11**. 1
subministrare **4**. 10
subsellium **16**. 9
substantia **1**. 32; **4**. 9, 21
substringere **1**. 32
successus **4**. 3
sufferentia **4**. 20, 25; **29**. 9
aquam sumere **13**. 7
superducere **1**. 9
superponere **11**. 11
superstitio **15**. 4
superstitiose **13**. 6
superstruere **10**. 5
supplere **1**. 7
supplicare **8**. 3
suspendere **3**. 21
suspensio **5**. 5
sustinere (=pati) **4**. 13, 16

terrenus **1**. 19, 20
testimonium **2**. 1
transfigurare **22**. 60
transigere **13**. 5
transire **1**. 18
tutela **9**. 7

vacare (=orba esse) **22**. 40, 41
valere **1**. 11
velle (=malle) **4**. 8; **7**. 7
veneratio **1**. 34
venia **7**. 5
veritas (i.e. Christus ipse) **28**. 7;
  29. 1
vetustas **1**. 10
via **11**. 1, 8, 9
vibrare **29**. 30
victima **7**. 3
virgines masculi **22**. 31
virgo, mulier, femina **21, 22** *passim*
voluntariae **22**. 78
voluntas **4**. 1 *et saepius*; **22**. 86

www.ingramcontent.com/pod-product-compliance
Ingram Content Group UK Ltd.
Pitfield, Milton Keynes, MK11 3LW, UK
UKHW042150280225
455719UK00001B/243